Living on Love

More books by
The Author
Klaus J Joehle

♥

Living on Love
"The Messenger"

♥

A Weekend With 'a'
Drunken Leprechaun

♥

Roberta's Coffee Table Book of Love
"Just Another Stuffed Poet"

Living on Love

✳

"The Shameful Secret" (The Rest of The Story)

We are not alone and neither are we powerless

Klaus J Joehle

Writers Club Press

San Jose New York Lincoln Shanghai

Living on Love
"The Shameful Secret" (The Rest of The Story)

Writers Club Press
an imprint of iUniverse, Inc.

For information address:
iUniverse, Inc.
5220 S. 16th St., Suite 200
Lincoln, NE 68512
www.iuniverse.com

ISBN: 0-595-22827-5

Printed in the United States of America

Love

To my sweetheart who obviously is the greatest
angel of them all
It's a very beautiful experience to have you in my
life
And very inspiring to know that you could love a
man
Who is as stubborn as a mule and draws his sword
Every time a leaf flutters to the ground
Angels bask in the light that shines from within you.

Thank you
For being in my life

Contents

A Word

I suppose in my own words that I believe in the possibility of truth more that truth itself. What holds true today falls aside in the light of tomorrow's truth.

Are truths not just a journey? Perhaps a journey with no end! Perhaps truth is just a fantasy we cling to for safety from the unknown, the things we can not fathom think that truth is closer to those inner sanctuary's, faith and trust then truth itself.

Having said that, the words I want to believe; so please make it true as I wish not to be fooled, unfold as a small quiet voice from somewhere deep in my mind. Yes, I see your point I answered back but truth is not mine to control neither yours.

Matter of fact as time passes, I become older I become less sure of everything except that time passes, and I am getting older. In my first book, I said I write the truth as best as I could. Now here in this book I must say I write what I believe is the possibility of truth.

If a story really ever ends or truly has a beginning; then here is as per say the rest of the story. As always, take what you like and leave the rest for someone that will love it.

All my love

Life is a matter of choice
We can choose Love or Sword and a billion choices in-between
Perhaps you have already decided
Or
Perhaps you have decided to wait and see what your enemy will do.

Considering the way the universes works if this book has come into your hands this story will either touch you in some way; or even be a part of your never ending journey.

Spelling and Grammar?

Bad spelling is like a beautiful flower
On the side of the road
Where it should not be
But takes you away from where
You should not have been going.

Missing punctuations
Are like angels you know
Should be there
But can't see them
That's why you think of them.

—*Klaus Joehle*

Foreword

A Few Words before We Start

In truth, it has taken a long time to write this book. Sometimes I am afraid of the truth, sometimes I don't want the truth to be the truth, and at the same time, there are times I'm ashamed of my truth.

This book will be difficult for you to read and so I would like to explain to you some of how this world and our universe works. I feel it will help you to understand what has happened and why things seem all over the place and why several things were happening at the same time. When you first mix light and darkness together, you get confusion you find yourself swung into a place of unknown uncertainty of what you are and how you are. Some of you will already have experienced this.

To start with, as I was writing my first book I was working with love and trying to write about it so others could see what was possible but at the same time there was also a darker side to me trying to settle a timeless old score, which has nothing to do with love. Although the first book is true, I left out much of the truth about what I had become and what I had done to myself with all my experiments. I had begun to open the door to love and to that loving part of myself; but also had opened the door to that other part of myself that dark part of myself that could kill and feel nothing of it. Each time I sit down to write this book I just physically begin to shake, my body gets ice cold no matter how hot it is. Some masters would say that it is best to leave some doors unopened but if you have read my other books then you know I could never leave those doors alone. I have some fear and I have some shame but I have no regrets. I think that some of my shame comes from the fact that I would do many of the things I did again. It was a journey I had to take regardless of the cost to myself and to others. They say they're are no victims and sometimes I would like to believe that just to make myself feel better; but it comes with great difficulty and I fear myself using it as an excuse as to what I have done. Look at it this way some say that we have lived other life times, that is fine but as you search further you realize that these other so called life times are actually happening now at this moment. Once you open those doors, you cannot close them and you become what you are in those other life times, you bring it into this life that's the danger or the glory.

It is a real danger, it almost killed me and almost turned me back into the darkness I had hoped to change. If in other lifetimes other probabilities you are doing good that's all fine its not that hard to take but if you open doors that say do not open under any circumstances then there is a reason a good reason. So what do you think would happen to you if you open those doors to find out that you are in fact the darkest evil that you at this time are trying to stop. How would you feel to find you are the ugliest that has ever roamed this earth and you find you cannot close the door and the more it stays open the more you become that. For what I am there and what I am here, are both melting into each other? If I would not have learned the art of sending love and how to use that power I would not have survived. The battle is not over how can I win a battle with myself. All I can hope for is that one can see the light of the other and by that hope that we both survive.

Unfortunately, life does not always unfold like the pages of books or like stories in books. It's a whole different story when you are living it. This book was difficult to write and will in its own way be difficult to read. Life can be simple and joyful but when you can't seem to leave no stone unturned, well then things can get a little hairy and confusing. I could have changed the story in this book into a make believe story that follows a certain order but in doing so it would not have been the truth and worst of all it would be very confusing to someone going through some of those things. It would look so different from what really happens as you start opening those mysterious doors. Life does not necessarily hand you things in a nicely written orderly fashion. It comes as it comes Sometimes you get the egg before you know what a chicken is. Many people write me of things that they are experiencing and they say that they cannot find any reference to these things in books and so feel lost. That is because books are written to be books not to explain the impossible or really show you what experiencing the impossible will put you through. Unfortunately as you hunt for the truth and search in those hidden places things sometimes come at the same time almost like you are living two life's at the same time and it seems that you are at two places at once. Nevertheless, how do you write being at two places at once and having two separate points of view at the same time when generally it is not even accepted that it is possible. I am also hoping that you can see that how we see reality is how our life's are formed. It is by what we see as truth is how we live and experience our lives.

If we look towards light we see light, if we turn around we see shadows. That should tell you something; see its something you never thought of is it? Its there every day and you don't see it but it affects everything you do and by not realizing that its there and what it means is that the experience you we have will be that of confusion. What this means is that we do not live in the light and we do not live in the darkness but we live where they meet right in the middle. Now you understand why it's all so confusing like they're are always opposing forces working one way as you go the other. Its an explosive place where its hard to tell with way is up. There is a balance and yet there is none. Best of all there is two of everything. When I say light and darkness I am not referring to good and evil just to two opposing forces of contrast. That's what makes this place so interesting it is seemingly built on and colossal contrast. The contrast exaggerates everything to enormity, but also makes everything bigger then it is. So, now that you know a little more of where you have chosen to experience life you can understand the turbulence; such a simple truth and it explains so much. Before I go on, I want to say something about light and darkness. Darkness is not evil or any less desired by all that is. It tries to convey that the light of the creator shines as bright in the darkness as it does in the light. Darkness is simply a contrast to see the light more clearly and light is simply a contrast to see the darkness more clearly. Both where created with the same love by all that there is. Person's actions have nothing to do with light or darkness they are simply actions. There is no more evil in the darkness then there is in the light. Matter of fact only love exists in true darkness as only love exists in true light. Light and darkness both sits in the creator's lap both created with the same love the creator creates everything with. So, you might ask where are we; are we in the light? Are we in the darkness? This is where the true magic lies. Magic is the love of asking, of searching and of creating consciously that what we want to experience and how we will experience it and to what degree it will challenge us to grow beyond any concept of limitations.

We have conditioned ourselves so much that whenever something bad happens we say it must be from the darkness and could not come from the light. This is even believed to such an extent that when some travel further into the light and they find something that is not so seemingly nice that they automatically assume it must be coming from the darkness and that they are not as far into the light as they have thought. This is incorrect and believing this will make your traveling into the light very confusing. The same goes the other way you can travel into the darkness and find just as much love there. You will just not see light that is all, but you can find the creator there as much as anywhere. So now you can see that us living in where light and darkness come together can be confusing because you are in fact sort of living two life's at the same time. When calm waters and a flowing river come together, you get turbulent waters of clear and muddy mixing together to form something new but ever changing. It is this mixing that creates what is seen nowhere else. That's what makes this place so special, so confusing and ever changing always in total contrast and it is this contrast that brings out the real beauty of both. Now in time the flowing water will shift as do all things and so in time the area that was in the turbulence will be in the darkness of muddy rich waters or become light of calm clear waters. Do you see the picture now; in time, we will be in the light that is the direction we are going. However, the elusion is that this will bring peace it is an elusion. We will have peace but not because of the light, it is natural to always change to something we are not, or to gravitate to the opposite. It is from the turbulence that we now desire calm; and it is our desires for calmness that will bring about peace. Now when you work with love as I have explained in my first book you will shift yourself into those calm waters by first creating calmness in yourself and by that shifting into calmness. In a sense the clear calm waters of light, Not every one will go that direction some will with love go to the calmness of darkness; there is also a third option. As the darkness meets with the light the turmoil of two energies, converging creates another place or better said an opening to…come on now at this point you should be able to tell me what this place is, what doorway does it open?

Ok! OK! I will tell you but as soon as I do you'll say I know that. As I explained with light and darkness what happens when those energies meet, this happens in everything with everything everywhere in the world with nature in the universe and everything that was created. Everything and every form of energy has its opposite and I mean everything; right down to the atom. So now, there will always be what we call a place where these opposing things meet.

This is so even with people. Each time these forces meet, there is a reaction, an energy created a vortex of sorts. Now I should tell you that light and darkness meet not only here where we live but also in other places. Each place will be a bit different but one thing does stay constant a sort of vortex is formed and does open. Now you think life in where we are is confusing and ever changing this vortex for a better word for it makes this look like a piece of cake.

OK! So I hope you are still with me. So now think about this all that we do whatever it is, all this activity be it even just an atom causing the creation and changing of what we could usually call energy but it's more than that. Therefore, in using an analogy you could say the creator creates and what he creates also then creates just the same as it works for us. We create a generator, this is converted to electricity, and that is converted to something that creates something else like smelting steel. So the creator creates and what he/she creates does also create. Do you see it? So lets say an enlightened fish comes to understand the dam and that it creates energy for those that created it. However, he/she cannot yet see what is done with this energy but sees the dam and the generator as sort of a vortex and if he follows the wires of electricity though where it goes he sees the creators, US humans creating things with this energy. So he/she might say oh, these are the creators that created the rivers and the dams and all that is. That is just an elusion. These vortexes will in a sense lead you to…something but it is not the creator but only a larger form of the creation for the fact is the creation you see and we are is the creator for the creator creates itself much as humans and all life seek to recreate itself. So, if you want to go home if you want to see the creator then look inside yourself, they're inside your heart; you will find an enormous spark of endless power to create anything; I call it Love. Therefore, as you work with love you walk hand in hand with the creator and are in a sense of the word home. Home is not so much a place as it is an act. It is when we create in the image of the creator you could say we are at home, that is home. When you open that valve of love inside your opening, in the way I explained in my other book. You are opening the flow of the creator, in fact he/she is then flowing thru you freely, and you will have in your hands an endless source of power to create whatever fancies you have, your joy your love. Does it all now make sense? I hope it does. But! There is more we are not done yet.

In order to truly create would it not help to understand some of what was already created? Of course, it would, to put it all into some temporary form of understanding from where we can expand our understanding. Sometimes but not always, it is easier to understand how something works by first taking it apart and then re-assembling it. You will know very fast if you understood it because if you did not fully understand the principle then you will soon find that it does not work. OK! So lets go on to the next thing.

So the idea that the world was flat came from some old writings that explained that world upon worlds are layered like stone layers. Alternatively, you could say a gigantic stack of papers each paper is a world very similar to yours but just a little different. In other words, there is no time, it is time that gives the elusion of movement but in fact, we live in a form of endless probable realities layered like paper and spreading out like a four-dimensional spider web. Ok! You can see the difficulty in explaining it but lets try it in several forms. Some of you might be familiar with a TV show called sliders where a scientist found a way to access these probable worlds and is now traveling from one to the next trying to get back to the one he thinks he came from. Of course in the TV show he thinks that none of the worlds he goes to, are as good as the one he came from. However, other then that he could stay where he is where he had made different choices and so has lived a different life.

So keep this in mind as we go on, also keep the following in mind. We create and then set about perfecting what we create but first we create and that is also how the creator creates he/she creates and then set out to perfect what is created and that is in fact what we are doing with our lives. Each life we set out to perfect what is already created; so in fact everything that is already created everything you can think of already is and what we now do is perfect it, like an artist we color in the blanks. So what that means is that the past still exists and the future also exists but all exists in the endless possibilities that where there and we flow inside of those endless variations perfecting each one of them more and more. Therefore, you could travel into the future and into the past of that reality you have experienced or into a billion variations of the future. Now as it goes each moment is one of those sheets of paper. The entire world as you see it is on it. But it is only one possibil-

ity of billions of what could be in endless variations. So lets say you go
into the past and give yourself the lottery numbers; in the theory that
some have, you would come back into the future and find that you are
rich. But that is not how it works you could travel into the future
where you are rich because of something you did but you could also go
into the present moment where you have endless probable possibilities
where in fact you are rich and that part of you has experienced a memory of how you became rich. OK so lets say you found a way to shift
right now to a reality that is playing right now where you are rich what
you would find is just that, but you would also have all the memories
associated with that experience and you would not remember coming
from the other reality. This is set up that way because it would get very
confusing of having two memories with two different outcomes. There
is a barrier in your mind that separates each memory so that it will not
become confusing and at the same time not drive you crazy. See you
cannot go into the future unless it is already there so you could not pre-
dict the future unless it is already there. So lets say you are predicting
the future, what you are doing is guessing at what probable world you
will be experiencing. So lets say someone says you will win the lottery
tomorrow in fact if you can think it then it has already happened but
will you shift into the world with that possibility set in; that's the thing
if you do you will experience winning if you do not you will not win.
Now the trick is to know how to shift in those probabilities, but that is
not something you want to do until you understand the implications
of what will happen to you and how it will affect your life. It is something that happens very naturally every day to everyone. We do not
notice it because we also switch memories and time is what makes that
possible. Time is what makes you think and makes it appear as if something just happened when in fact it already was. Sometimes we do take
some memories with us and that is when we get the feeling that we did
something like go to the store when in fact we did not go and yet we
can clearly remember going to the store. Now you're getting it! Sometimes as people get old, they talk about things that happened in the

past and people around them say that this is not how it happened. This happens when that barrier in your mind breaks down and releases memories of other probabilities that were played out. So it is that they begin to access those probabilities while still staying in the one they are in, sometimes they then will shift over to that probability. Now you would say if that is so then why can we, here in this probability still see them. Because there is no time and so, you are everywhere all the time; it is time that gives you the elusion of separation.

So the next question would be can you prove this to yourself, O' yes you can. But do you want to? The price can be high especially if you are just starting out and have no idea what will happen and are crazy enough to do things that is said not to do, then your story might unfold as mine did as you will see if you keep on reading. I wanted to understand I did not care what the price was or the cost to me or to anyone else. So that's how I got into the mess I got myself into. There is a way to shift and do it in such a way that it enriches your life and even others and there is a way to be fully aware of it all and stay sane. I was young and impatient and did not see what was in store for me until after I was way over my head, but then that's nothing new. If you continue your working with love as I have set out in my first book your ability to casually shift in all the probabilities will come to you naturally, slowly but naturally. Here is one more thing this is something that I did not see for a long time. As you get good at sending love and working with love you will begin to shift in the probabilities effortlessly and joyfully but even better, you will in fact change that probability to something better. As you can imagine it would take an enormous force or power to change what already is created but when you work with Love did, I not tell you that the creator is then flowing thru you.

O' we are not finished with this yet. Science is slowly realizing the atom can actually be at more then one place at the same time. The implications of that can seem staggering but that is just an elusion of time. There are only two atoms in your body, what we could call positive and negative remember light and darkness coming together creating a vortex of sorts that is your body it is the two atoms in close combination creating a vortex and in time creating billions of them that's how two atoms form your body. Therefore, you can sort of see how you can be everywhere and shift easily. This is of course an extremely simplified example and so at the same time incorrect.

OK! So let's finish up with how the different possible realities bleed into each other and some of the affects it has on us even when we are not aware of it. So you have so many probable worlds and all so close together and each being just the tiniest bit different or totally different, before I say any more remember this. You have chosen to be where you are even if you can't remember choosing. Therefore, at this time, there are probable worlds already at peace and there are probable worlds at war and some almost destroyed. Every probability you can imagine exists. Now the really neat part is that we naturally shift around in these probable worlds every day un-knowingly and unaware of it. So you wonder when you put something somewhere and come back later to find it somewhere else what is happening. See the probable worlds can be so close that you can hardly tell the difference unless you are extremely observant. I know, now that I mentioned this some of you would start saying, oh now I see what is happening; now the things that I have seen are starting to make sense.

Well there is something more to think about! Remember at the beginning I said that we are living in the vortexes of light and darkness converging. This causes enormous energy rifts and you might say throwing things a little out of balance. The end result is that the different probable worlds are bleeding into each other. This is the fun part. In our world, there is so much confusion of what is or is not everyone seems to believe something else and feels they have proof of it and yet can't prove it to someone else. This is because of the different worlds bleeding into each other but in a jumbled sort of way. I will try to explain it this way.

You and your neighbor can seemingly live in the same world but because of the bleed thru affect he or she is living in a different world just as real as yours but not visible to you as some of yours is not visible to him or her. Now you might believe in aliens and even have seen some, you could have your little toe shot off by one and have it on video. As you show it to your neighbor, they will see it as a fake and will find people of his reality that will prove it to be fake and you will find the ones in your reality that will prove it to be real. Confusing isn't it; well that's why we live in such confusing times, worlds and so on. Now if you have read my first book of sending love and that is real to you because that is the world you live in then you will find also people to whom this means nothing, because even though you can see them and they can see you they live in a reality where it does not exist. Its sort of like, I have a book of my reality and you have one of yours and we each take some pages out of each others books photocopy them and put them into each others books. So there will be certain things we will agree on like your car is blue but there are probable realities where your car is red and you will find some people who would swear your car was red, but now they see that your care is blue. It gets worse the probable worlds are mixing together and so causing this confusion but at the same time they are constantly shifting so different worlds are constantly mixing but at the same time it is not stationary they are constantly changing. So, what this means as in the example I gave you from exchanging pages in our books of our lives and our realities we constantly exchange. See the vortex is constantly mixing the worlds together but in an ever-changing way. I will try to give you an example. Sometimes someone will have said something to you and later they will say that they did not say this and will say that what they said was different. Now I'm not talking about people who lie but people you know and trust. I am sure that this will have happened to you because you will tell them that you heard them very clearly state that they liked something and now they are saying that they have never liked that whatever it may be. See that gets very confusing because you both feel you are right and in fact, you both are right. See if you believe in aliens and it is real to you it is probable because in your reality in your world they do exist and your neighbors is also right when he/she say's that they do not exist because in they're world that they live in there are no aliens at all. Both worlds are as real as the other and normally would not be combining in this way or colliding in this way. Now guess what! There is also a reality where your neighbor is believing in aliens and may even have seen them and is living in the same world as you but because of the vortexes we are in it is not what you are experiencing. However, here is the kicker; because of the vortexes one day, you could be speaking to your neighbor to find out that he/she believes in aliens. Then you will ask when did this happen, you never believed in aliens before and your neighbor will look at you like you are weird because he/she will say that she has always believed and say to you that you have discussed it many times. See the probability has shifted but your memories, which should also have shifted, did not. Normally your memories will shift as you shift around in the probabilities but because of the vortexes this is not always happening so you might shift and still remember it as it was before. Of course, you will think you are losing it but your not. Once you understand what is happening it easier to deal with and can be a lot of fun.

So lets take it one step further. So, you might feel as if this will go on forever. No it won't because the vortexes of light and darkness mixing is not a reality everywhere in every probability and some time you might slowly bit by bit shift into probabilities where that vortexes no longer exist. Now! Also, it seems that it depends where you live in the world at any particular place will also affect how strong these vortexes shift the probabilities around and mixes them. Some places are affected more so then others but that also changes from time to time. So with all of this some of you who have read my first book might ask how does sending love mix with this.

Well! Regardless where you are in whatever probability in whatever world you will have a power source. It may be more apparent to you in some and more hidden in others but it will always be there no mater what you call it. Because it is what you are without it/you would not exist. So what affect does sending love have on this vortex?

That is an easy one, first you need to remember that you wanted to be here and for good reason. It's quite the exciting place. Now sending love won't take you out of this unless that is your desire instead it will create a vortex of its own, that will bring the best of everything to you and you to it and by that giving you the most joyful life and experiences. It will attract the best to you at any given time. O' there is that word again *Time*...he's a bad one let me tell you. *Time* is the master of elusions. *Time* makes you think you did something yesterday when in fact you are doing it right now. So now, you can imagine if you start kicking in the closed doorways of *Time* that things could get a little hairy. So much so, that what might have been another lifetime in how we sometimes perceive things can in fact turn into this lifetime mixing with this life. You won't know if you are a barbarian dreaming you were and accountant or and accountant dreaming you were a barbarian. What happened? All of a sudden, the barbarian can count and the accountant wants to work on his savage attack plan. O' you see what's happening now don't you!

Shall I go on?

Introduction

Creating the life we want
Is a lot like carving stone
Any good sculptor
Knows that stone is not carved into a form
But that stone is removed too
Reveal the form that lies within

1

Summer of 2000, my wife Roberta went to Edmonton to visit her son. I decided to stay home to work on various things to do with love energy. I had already started on this book a year before but dropped it; I was totally unsatisfied with it. In my opinion, it wasn't serving any purpose. I was and have been working on something more elaborate and productive. At least in my opinion, as usual the universe was in disagreement with me. My guides said to finish telling the rest of the story before going on to what was next in the plan. They said that it would create the foundation for what was to come. Also, I had many people write me asking when I would tell the rest of the story. To me it is like old news. On the other hand coming to an understanding of the power of sending love is a journey, not the flick of a switch as I had hoped. Sometimes my impatience gets the best of me.

As I sat there re-reading what I had written I just decided to erase it all and go on a short trip to the mountains for some direction. I thought that I might go to a power spot not far from Calgary, Alberta. There is a large vortex there not unlike what you would find in Sedona. This spot is a little different but the same things apply. Its funny but people travel all over the world from here to visit special places and don't realize that they're within one hour of a very special and powerful place. It's just that it has been carefully hidden. People assume that some of the most powerful places in the world would be marked. Not likely, in fact just the opposite. No shaman would be foolish enough to mark these spots so that anyone could come there. The only time that happens is when a place has changed and is ready for people at large. By that time, shames will already have moved tier powers to another spot. If you went there, you might see what appears to be a tiny vortex, it is like that of an iceberg.

What's underneath would make most other vortexes seem puny. It's not for the faint of heart. I tell you more of how to get there and what to expect later. For now, let us get to the rest of the story.

After erasing most of what I had written, I drove out to this place. On the way, there I passed a certain gas station that had been closed for some years. This is the same gas station that I had spoken about in the beginning of my first book, Living on Love "The Messenger". You can read about what had happened there in that book so I won't go into it here.

While passing that gas station, I thought I should stop for something to eat as it was going to be a long hike to the place where I was heading. After parking, the car I went into the restaurant part of the gas station. It hadn't changed much. There where only a few people in the restaurant, mostly truck drivers having some coffee. I sat myself on one of the stools at the front counter. The waitress was talking to some of the truck drivers so I took a look at the menu that was laying there. Under the glass jar was what looked like a good homemade apple pie. Before the waitress even got to me, I decided on apple pie and hot chocolate. The waitress said goodbye to the truck drivers as they left. By the time, she came around the counter the people on the other table where getting up to leave also. My favorite way to sit in a restaurant, just me, I thought to myself.

"So what can I get you today darling?" Asked the waitress.

I recognized her instantly. It's not a face you can forget. The most unlikely looking angel you would ever see. "What a moron you are judging people by their looks" I said to myself. One day I'm going to rip that part of my brain right out of my head. Sometimes I can't stand myself. She wasn't ugly just more of a truck driver than an angel. I think that it was fear of being recognized and embarrassed that made my judgmental mind come forth like that. After all I owe her a lot for the kindness, which she had shown me a long time ago.

"I'll have some apple pie and some hot chocolate thank you," I answered sheepishly. The words I'm such an idiot, I'm such an idiot were running around in my mind to the point that it was turning into a musical all I needed was the dance of an idiot to complete the musicale and that I accomplished as soon as she had put the cup of hot chocolate in front of me.

"There you go darling," She said. Not only did I manage to spill it but also I managed to spill it all down her apron.

She laughed mostly at the forty shades of red on my face. The cook was looking thru the open window where the food was past thru. "Wahoo good one" he yelled my direction laughing

"I'm so sorry are you alright" I asked.

"That's ok Klaus," she answered.

"What! How do you know my know my name?" I asked while trying to help clean up.

"Come on now did you think I would forget, aren't you the one that was driving up and down the highway a few years ago."

"Ya that was me", I answered embarrassment level nine coming up

"So how do you know my name? Did I tell you my name?"

"Na About three or four weeks ago a couple of ladies came in here asking some questions. Also if I read your book?" She answered walking away to get more hot chocolate, while leaving me hanging.

She put the hot chocolate down way passed my reach and preceded to get my apple pie.

Mentally I sent her a message, big piece, big piece, big piece…

It worked; she brought back what looked like it could have been half the pie.

"There you go", she said then reaching for the hot chocolate. She set the hot chocolate down but still had her hands on it. My hands were on my lap waiting for permission.

With the other hand, she reached under the bar and pulled out a can of whip cream. If an alien came to my house and asked what two things, he should see while visiting. I would tell him chocolate and whip cream, or better yet both at the same time. It's what life is all about. It's what makes me tick.

She held the cup of hot chocolate and the whip cream hostage. Looked right at me and said, "*So what is the rest of the story?*"

I know if I messed around that there wasn't going to be any whip cream. Therefore, I answered with a question. "You want to know *the rest of the story.*" I asked

"You what some whip cream?" She asked still holding it hostage

"Ok" I said. "But how do you know about the book and what were those people asking about" I asked. I admit I was a little worried.

"Ed get your ass our here you are gonna want to hear this" She yelled. Almost scaring me to death.

I heard some dishes clang, one minute later I saw a man coming around the corner cleaning his hands on a dish rag well the waitress poured on the whip cream. It was stacked so high there was no hope of ever getting to the hot chocolate. More like a challenge. Just the way I like it. Yummy yummy in my tummy.

"What's up Sally" Ed asked while casually standing behind the waitress.

I could see that they're were spark's there; more then just co-workers. Ed had love in his eyes, no doubt about that.

"This is Klaus," answered Sally, pointing to me with excitement.

Ed reached out his hand; I lifted mine as we shook hands I could see in his eyes that he had no clue as to why I was being introduced.

This is the guy; you know the book, the guy that I told you about driving back and forth on the highway…the book that those ladies left here.

"No! Really you're the guy" answered Ed, wow what a great book, you know I would have had a hard time believing some of the stuff if it wasn't for Sally telling me the story about you driving up and down the highway

"Thanks, I think?" I said, shoving some pie into my mouth.

"He's going to tell us the rest of the story," said Sally

"I'm in for that," answered Ed. What perfect timing I'll get my stuff.

"What's perfect timing? How did you get the book? And what did those ladies want?" I asked shoving another piece of apple pie into my face. I knew it was going to be now or never.

Ed came flying around the corner at full speed carrying a stool. He sat the stool down flopping himself on it as if time was of the utmost importance.

"Perfect timing" Ed said, looking at sally.

"We are leaving for Sedona next week" answered Sally

"Why are you going there?" I asked.

Ed looked at Sally; Sally looked at Ed; Ed answered. "We just feel it's the right thing to do, its like we are sort of drawn there".

"We have been saving up for it for a while" responded Sally. We have been working on sending love for a while now too and ever since we just feel that, we should make the trip.

"Are you planning to live there?" I asked

"O' ya we want to stay for as long as it feels right" answered Ed

"I've always wanted to go there and see it," I answered it just hasn't been the time yet, but its defiantly is in the plan. So how's sending love going for you."

"Really well; answered Ed we have done a few experiments with it and had some real interesting results". Tell him Sally

"Actually I would like to know about those ladies and what they wanted" I interrupted

"O' they came in here asking some questions about a story they had heard about a guy that was driving up and down the highway. Sally was laughing now, I told them that I remembered that. At that point, they were really excited and wanted to know the whole story. I asked them why? And they showed me your book. It wasn't a book but a print out. They showed me the part where you write about it. Then I got pretty excited because I didn't know the whole story until then. When they were ready to go they left the book with me. They also had told me that they were going to try and find some special places in the mountains that they had heard you knew about. I don't know what that was about".

I dropped my fork. Sun of a...how did they find out about that? I mumbled to myself. They're going to get more than what they're bargaining for.

"Do you know who they are? Their names" I asked.

"First names only" Sally answered.

"Why what's the problem"? Asked Ed.

I grabbed my cup of hot chocolate and sucked up a pile of loving smooth whip cream.

"It doesn't matter now I guess it is what it is, can I give you a little suggestion, something to think about before you go to Sedona" I answered changing the subject.

"Shore" answered Ed and Sally nodded

"It's like this. I said. Before you go to Sedona and before you go to any power spots, it would be very beneficial if you focus on opening your hearts and sending love. The power spots will enhance those things that are important to you and the things that you are focusing on. This is why some people can't handle spending much time there. If some one has to many negative thoughts and believes, they will be enhanced in the same way. It will focus on what you focus on. Do you see what I mean? If you worry you'll have something to worry about. If you send love you'll have something to love and will attract more love."

"That's a good point," answered Ed.

"We have been working on sending love" answered Sally

"Just keep going with that; it will all work out for you. At least that's what I have found from my experiences."

We spent some time just talking back and forth for a while, as I ate my pie. I felt the universe had given me an opportunity to tell the rest of the story in much the same way as last time. So, I decided to accept the offer.

Bring Love

Show me a path that angels fear to tread
I may go in screaming,
I'll probably come out screaming
But no longer will I fear any path
For I only fall when I forget to bring Love

2

By the time I was ready to begin telling the rest of the story Ed had gotten Sally another stool for her. They seemed to mix well together; I liked them and wanted to give them something to begin their new journey with love. The gas station was busy but the restaurant was empty; several people had looked in but had left abruptly.

Rubbing my forehead I said, "We might as well start at the beginning". This story is a lot harder to tell than the first one. It's like when you ask a tree to tell you its story, it won't understand what you are asking because a tree is more than just branches a trunk and roots. Even though every branch and leaf is connected they are all experiencing different things, each branch, twig and leaf has a life of its own. The tree may be in the forest and the sun is shining in but not all the branches are receiving sunlight. Some are on the shady moist side and some on the sunny dry side. Some branches will feel the force of the storm well others hardly know that there is a storm. So depending on what the tree as a whole is focusing on will depend on the experience it is having. It's like that for people to. We can get fired from a job and feel and experience many different things all at the same time but it's the things that we mostly focus on that will form our memories. We can feel anger, betrayal, and fear, joy, freedom and hope for new possibilities all at the same time. I remember being let go from a job I didn't like but needed to have for the money. What I remember was a feeling of freedom and joy; I savored every moment. The weather was sunny and hot and I spent a lot of my time in the park enjoying the time and freedom to re-think my life. They're where struggles but I don't remember them because I was not focusing on them at all. That's where sending love really shines because by doing that you would be focusing on positive things and positive possibilities. Even without what love can do it would already become a more positive situation. Then you add the possibilities of love working for you and soon you have a very loving experience what could have been devastating. "Do you see what I am saying"? I asked.

"Ya focus and send love and that's what we will find," answered Ed.

"Not only that but that's what we will remember" answered Sally.

"Some things are dramatic enough, I said; that there's only one way to see them. Like when a branch is ripped off in a storm. Those are also the things that form how we see the world and our lives. How our experiences form our personalities. About the only thing that can heal those scars and prevent more things like that from happening is love and forgiveness. That leaves us with two types of experiences; the ones where we can see them as opportunities to see the best in what might not appear to be the best and the type of experiences where we need to have love and forgiveness to survive them in order to not have them affect the rest of our lives".

There was a moment of silence before I continued.

The first thing we need to discuss is my inability to write. "That's right; I said I can't spell at all. I can read fluently but not write, at least not in an earth language. I have not been able to figure out what purpose it serves for me to be able to write in a language that no one but me can read, but that is the way it is". Ed was going to say something but I just continued.

Over time I have tried to learn to write but it seems even my abilities to learn are blocked. Rather strange, don't you think? Especially since my mission in this life was to write two or three books on the topic of sending love. This is what I mean; my not being able to write is like a branch of my life. But not one I was born with, it was one that came after.

"That's something that I always found strange about life," added Sally. My mother always said that you would find you gifts in the same box as you challenges.

"That's a good point and so true" responded Ed

"Where did the spelling problem come from"? Asked Sally

"What about the other language"? Asked Ed

"Wow slow down one thing at a time" I responded

"Ya let him tell the story," said Sally poking Ed, which turned into a poking match by two people who can't keep their hands of each other.

I waited for them to finish their playful teasing and the continued.

See it's hard to say if my spelling problem is a broken branch or an added branch. The full verdict is not in yet. So far, my inability to write has caused me a lot of trouble and has never gone over well in the work place. As you can imagine moving up the ladder could be a problem. There is a reason for my inability to write and I guess this is where we should start this story on how all of this got started. The other language that I am fluent in is a very complex language and it would take a long time to learn but it is just there. Once I explain where the spelling problem came from you might come to the same conclusions that I have as to how I ended up able to write in another language. This other language is in symbols and each symbol is stories as per say. By arranging the symbols and thus the stories in a certain order, it creates a new story the one you are trying to convey. It is complicated but yet simple, 24 lines of 4 to 8 symbols in each line would explain this book. In other words, this book could fit on a business card.

I stopped to sip some of my hot chocolate and lit a cigarette.

Ed reached behind himself for an ashtray, which he proceeded to place in front of me. I thought that as an ok for me to smoke.

"Anyway so here we go," I said. I was born in Germany Freiburg on September 24, 1957. Later my parents moved to a tourist town, called Titisee in what is called the Black Forest. There they bought a hotel; if you were to ask twenty people why it is called Black Forest you could get twenty different answers right from simple logical ones, as the trees are too black don't go there at night. To me the forest was an incredible place of peace, mystery and adventure. They're were things there I could not understand but accepted as is. The trees, the mystery of the forest was all I needed; that forest, those trees were safety and love to me and also my friends. As it was, those trees were my only friends. People were very superstitious and in my opinion very strange, even though they did not think of themselves as such. The town of Titisee could be as quiet as a calm lake one moment and as busy as a beehive the next, depending on the influx of tourists. The town and the surrounding area were mostly hotels smaller tourist shops and farmers. In some ways, it was modern but in other ways, it resembled medieval times. Some of the population had money while others had very little. The business owners drove Mercedes and the farmers still milked cows by hand and collected crops like hay and potatoes by hand barely making a living. It was as if two worlds were wrapped in one, some peoples main concern was where to vacation in the quiet times and others hoping to be able to pay the land taxes. Business people lived in fancy places while others lived in places that would bring you back two hundred years in time. For some people, their houses, pig barns, cow shelters and chicken coups were all one building. You could open a kitchen door and have the pigs standing in the pen waiting for leftovers right there in the next room. This was all very strange to me and confusing at best. For some reason even as I am telling you this, I can still smell those barn smells that lingered in their homes.

"When I was overseas with the army I had seen a lot of that; said Ed directing it towards Sally as she was making some funny faces.

"There are still places like that today; not as many though" I answered back and continued. At the time I'm speaking of, I was between the ages of 6 to 7 years old. My parents were hotel owners and worked from early morning until late at night. Closing only as the last guest had gone to bed. By this time mother had become very sick. At the time, I did not understand what cancer was. She was either in the hospital or sick in bed. That meant my father had even more work on his hands; so, I grew up without parental supervision and very little if any influence from television. This had a very bazaar affect on me. There are many things we learn from others beginning at an early age. The implications are quite staggering. Many people have come to the conclusions that children have certain talents that are later suppressed by outside influences. If you remove those influences then things can be quite different. I saw the world from my own eyes and thoughts, uninfluenced by what others had come to believe. I was able to accept or reject what I saw and witness without any influence of what a parent or society would have you believe. It set me apart and made me an outsider. If a child is raised, by a parent that believes certain things regardless if they are truth or not there is a high probability that the child will accept these things also. Sometimes without question, without those influences I saw things quite differently. My actions nor my behavior, nor my thinking pattern was modeled after anyone or by anyone.

I stopped for a minute grabbed a napkin and wrote these words down as they were flowing into my thoughts.

> *It seems that in the dark crevasses of our minds there linger thoughts that we dare not speak or act upon for ear of reprisal of others. There are also things we dare not believe for the same reasons. Sometimes we create that which we believe after we have been convinced that it is the truth and there by creating it to be the truth when in fact it is nothing more than an elusion of the truth. We can become so convinced that even when evidence of the opposite is there we refuse to see it. Sometimes we become convinced that it is better to live a lie than to face the hardship of truth. That is something we all know to well. But by living that lie we pass it on to our children. That is a crime that I to am guilty of even though I know better.*

After writing it out I read it back to Ed and Sally.

"Do you always write things down as they come to you"? asked Sally.

"I try to; I said answering back you never know if it's useful. If you get it written down and get a chance to look at it some time later".

Anyway getting back to the story, I suppose because of my independence and need to fend for myself I began rejecting most everything I heard from others. I had no friends at all. The wealthy did not want their children playing with me because I was not controllable and did not see value in what they had. Parents of poor families did not want me playing with their children either but mostly due to fear and superstition, for some reason they thought I was something evil or whatever. I could see it in their eyes and their actions at times they where almost afraid of me and yet lost as to why. There was the odd person that had showed me kindness but seldom and limited to who else was watching.

"Strange isn't it? I said in some ways it was almost like living in the dark ages".

Regardless I moved along quite happily spending most of my time in the woods or at the lake. I did have what you might call an invisible friend; I have explained this in my first book but unfortunately, I cannot elaborate on this friend or our interaction. The memories are just too vague and there are only bits and pieces flashes and glimpses. I know there was more, but at this moment, the door to that part of my mind is closed. I have kicked it and banged on it but it refuses to open. So, for now I'll leave this and go on with the rest as I remember it.

I asked sally for some water and waited for her before continuing.

Because of my parents being busy running the hotel and of course my mother being very sick I had total freedom to travel where ever I wanted and do whatever I wanted to do. I don't think it bothered me to be alone, besides I was not totally alone. Looking back now I can remember that I felt like I was being watched, perhaps even taken care of, I could feel it and sense it especially in the woods. One of the first incidences that come to mind was when I took a wagon home that I found in the woods; it was a big wagon for hauling firewood and had big wooden wheels. I wasn't trying to steel it just borrow it for a while. It seemed the perfect wagon to go down hill with and I had the perfect hill in mind. It was a long narrow road right beside our hotel, very steep but straight, well almost. This was not a one-day plan and it took careful planning. A half a day to get the wagon to the hill and up it, then to ride it down several times and then to return it the next day.

I headed out early in the morning to retrieve the wagon. While dragging it through the woods, I kept getting shivers up my spine.

Stopping many times to look around, seeing nothing I continued on my journey.

Eventually after getting it to the destination on top of the hill I was preparing to ride it down as a boy named Richard came along. I had seen him many times on my travels and thought that he might want to be friends with me but I think he was a little scared of being seen with me. He asked me what I was doing and I proceeded to explain it to him with great excitement of what fun it was going to be. While I had made my first sale and he wanted to come along. Jumping into the wagon, I told him to sit in the back and run the brakes and I would do the steering. After explaining how to use the stick I gave him as brakes by rubbing it against the tire we where off. Our speed went past my expectations and all previous tests. The speed became a problem perhaps because of the extra weight and the brakes were pretty much useless. Even though our speed had increased to such a level that Richard needed to toss the brakes just to be able to hang on, the next problem was coming along a lot faster then anticipated; steering was having very little affect. The wooden wheels were surrounded with a layer of steel where they made contact with the pavement. I turned the wheel turned towards the small patch of grass at the end of the road just before it ran into the main highway the wheels were not griping. Even if they had it would not helped much at this speed for there would be no way to stop once we reached the short patch of grass. The patch of grass was just a short patch leading to an embankment that dropped straight on to the highway. There was no time left for anything except to accept things as they are. Not a moment to soon the wheels started to grip and we were turning. Twenty feet on to the grassy patch the wagon came to a sudden halt. It didn't just stop; the front wheels locked and the cart tilted upwards catapulting us out like rockets. We were in the air for at least another twenty feet but for some reason Richard seemed to pass me in mid air and hit the ground a split second before me actually cushioning my fall because I landed on top of him. After picking ourselves up, I walked to the wagon to see what stopped it there was nothing there not even a rock. The wagon path was completely clear of obstruction. Richard just stood where he had landed and would not come any closer to the wagon. Pushing the wagon back and forth, I said it was fine; Richard turned and walked away. Obviously this was not the day for new alliances or friendships, all because a slight miscalculation.

"There could be a reason why you had no friends"; Interrupted sally laughing holding her head as if there was a disaster in the making.

"Could happen to anyone! Answered Ed smiling, wish I were there".

"My sediments exactly"! I said.

"You could have been killed!" Responded Sally.

"Ah! Whatever..." I said shrugging it off. Regardless, 1 to 2 years later we did become friends for a brief moment in time. From what I had heard, he became an electrician and has a family of his own. Sometimes I wonder what his side of the story would sound like. It would not have been the same with out him!

"Well I bet you won't do that again," Answered sally.

"To late did it with my son; I said he still talks about it today. Calls it the day my dad took me flying. Nevertheless, that's another story for another time.

I wish

O' star so bright
The first star I see tonight
I wish I may wish I might
To have the dream
I LoveD last night

3

A fter sally calmed down, I continued with the story.

Although there where many strange things that occurred in the woods this was the first of a four incidences that I can put into words. Before we go on to a really bazaar incident I can tell you about one strange place in the woods. There was a small pond where I spent a lot of time. At one end of the pond, there was a trail with many trails used but hardly anyone would ever go to the other end of the pond. I personally spent a lot of time there and felt safer then at home. One particular time some kids were chasing me and wanted to beat me up. They had chased me for a long time but the woods were my home and I know them well. The chase continued until I made it to the end of the pond and that is as far as they would go. They would take a few steps but then quickly retreat. I know that would happen because many people thought that it was haunted.

I never saw anything other than perhaps out of the corner of my eyes but I could feel something and sense it. Years later as I learnt remote viewing and I discovered that at that time there was a small race of beings that had lived there for a long time. Unfortunately, they have long left. They are many more things that went on in those woods. Also, I do remember having what some might call an invisible friend that I spent time with in the woods but the door to those memories are shut tight. What I do remember are some pieces to small to make head or tales out of, as if looking thru a keyhole I can see that I was having long conversations with someone but how or what was said is closed. Personally, I think that now would be a good time to remember so I can write it out and be done with it. I am positive that there was a lot more going on in the woods at that small pond. Even later in my life as

I learned to remote view most of what went on there was blocked. I could tell that there where beings living there perhaps as many as sixty but I could not interact with them. They knew I was there looking but would not acknowledge my presence. Therefore, for now I will tell you of what I remember, I think that will be enough to swallow for the time being. Perhaps I don't really want to remember. Perhaps that's a clue of why some memories are blocked. Or maybe not.

"What's remote viewing" asked Ed

It is a way of going somewhere to see what is there with your mind without taking your body. It is something like traveling out of your body but more common and a lot easier to learn. You can read about it on the Internet. It is very common. Anyway, I left my dog in the car and he is probably wondering where I am. I'm going to let him run around for a bit then we can continue.

"Why don't you bring him in"? Asked Ed

"Well I don't want to cause you trouble".

"Na; as long as he sits quietly somewhere no one will even notice".

"Fine with me" I said getting up.

I let Roody run around for a while, gave him some water, and then brought him in. he found himself a corner and flopped down content with life as usual.

Together with Love

Together with Love
We stand
For the whole is stronger
Than its parts
Together as one
With love and trust
We stand
Against the fears of the
Past, present, future
Love bends us beyond foolish temptation of fears
Our love is what gives us strength
Our love gives us trust
Our Dreams give us
The life we have
Wanted for so long
As we allow us to become One but Individual
We grow beyond our Dreams
So it is

4

"**I** think he's a little upset at not going for a walk but I told him we'll go tomorrow," I said to Ed and Sally.

"Have you had him for a long time" Asked Ed.

"O' ya since the holy terror of puppy hood, I said, I am not even going to get into that".

He is so relaxed! Responded Sally, you're probably exaggerating".

"Ya you go with that; the two of us know better" I answered while Roody waged his tail as if to say its all in a days work. I love you and to show you how much I missed you I will eat your house.

After we rambled back and forth for a while I suggested that it is a long story and if they wanted to hear it, we need to get back to it. Everyone agreed so I continued.

"What comes next will be a little weird and will probably raise a lot of questions; I said regardless I will not answer any questions regarding it so you will need to come to terms with it for yourself".

Sally and Ed both nodded their heads in agreement, but probably a little leery of what was coming.

It was the summer of my turning seven, I was returning home from my usual expeditions. I decided to take a short cut thru an area I did not usually like. It was a pathway between two rows of houses. The path was mostly straight except for two sharp turns. Both sides of the path were lined with very high and thick hedges. All you could se was the path. The reason I did not like it was that I could get trapped there because there was only one way in and one way out. Also because of the sharp turns it made I could not tell how or what I was going to run into. One time I was trapped in-between two mean dogs they were snarling and showing their teeth and coming closer, looking like they were going to attack. There was no place for me to go the hedge was too thick and there was no way of passing the dogs. I had tried to go towards in hope that it would back away but it just moved in closer and became more vicious. It was what seemed like a long time before someone came to scare them away. The person that came to help was an old man. He seemed to appear out of nowhere standing beside me. I saw him only a few times in my life.

"The old man in the bar you talked about in the book" Asked Sally.

"Ya; I answered but we will get to that shortly". As soon as the old man showed up the dogs took off with their tail between their legs. As soon as the dogs left I was out of there without a word. That incident scared me enough that I would never take that path again. It was totally out of the ordinary for animals to behave that way towards me. Plus I had never seen those dogs before.

The only reason for me to take that path this time again was that it was a short cut home. I was hungry and tired so I decided to take another chance. As I cautiously approached the pathway, I stopped to look and listen for anything or anyone. The coast seemed clear. I started of slowly and quietly then began to speed up as I past the first turn all you can see is hedges no entrance nor exit not until you pass the next turn. I heard a loud high-pitched sound that hurt my ears. I placed my hands over my ears and must have closed my eyes for a second because when I opened them I was somewhere else.

At that time in my life, I had never heard of aliens or space ships. I had never even seen anything on TV as to that existing. However, what I had heard of was elves and I had heard many people mention them, although I don't remember ever seeing any of them. I have had people say to me or ask me if I was afraid of the elves and witches.

So there, I was still holding my hand over my ears but standing in front of what I thought was an elf. I just stood there, looking at him and glancing around at where I was. The elf was about the same height as me but funny looking. He had clothes on something like that of nuns or priests, but not white nor black. Dark green like that of a tree. The best way to describe him is to say he looked like an alien described as grays. If you have seen pictures of them just think of them a little shorter and stockier, shorter neck and smaller eyes. Although his eyes were very large in comparison to mine and very dark almost black but not black. No hair on his face or on his head but he did have pointy cheeks unlike some of the pictures I have seen of what grays supposedly looked like. The room was shiny metallic like that of mag wheels but there was no reflection. He put out his hand to shake hands. I let go of my ears but didn't touch him. Nothing about him or the room I was in seemed threatening. He told me that everything is ok and he wanted to be my friend. I suppose that might have been the magic word. There were no words I heard him in my head. However, I heard him loud and clear. He moved over to a table not much higher then a chair and asked me if I would sit here, pointing with his long bony fingers. I didn't mind him nor how he looked but I did not like his hands. They looked too much of what you could call hands of a witch. He must have understood and seemed to let his sleeves slide over his hand so all I could see was his fingers. Without question, I went to sit on the table. As I moved my feet seemed to be sticky on the floor, just enough so you could not slide them. He talked to me for a while asking me things like if I was still afraid of those dogs. Then he began to explain where I was and who he was. Even though it did not make a lot of sense to me, he still tried to explain. He said that he was from the stars that you could see at night and that we were in a ship that could fly from star to star. He said that he came to help me and wanted to change something in me. Then he asked if that was ok. I sort of said ok. However, it was as if he did not ask me he seemed to ask something in me and I could sense that something in me said ok. Looking at it from what I know to day; I would say he was asking a larger part of me for permission, perhaps my soul or higher self. I myself trusted him, for some reason I did not get any negative feelings from him and there was a feeling that he really cared. That is not what I got from other people. Therefore, in a sense it was nice. A door opened but it was not a door it was like a piece of the wall disappeared. Two others like him came in and I could see thru the opening in the wall that there were others sitting around a pedestal of light or something in that affect. The two that came in spoke to me but I do not remember what was said, most likely just friendly stuff to keep me at ease. They went to the backside of the table where I was sitting. He told me that I would need to sit very still and not to move my head. He said that a few times and each time I nodded my head until I finally caught on to that I was moving. He seemed amused by that and I know it was keeping me busy while the others were doing something behind me. I asked if it was going to hurt because if it does I am out of here. He said no. They put something into the back off my neck and I could feel it going down my spine wrapping itself around my spine. There was no pain and he kept talking to me saying that it was fine. He was asking me questions about sword fighting, which I did a lot of using sticks of course. But the fact that he had interest is what was important to me. I was thinking that I might have a friend. Whatever went down my neck was left there, that was also, what he said. Then he asked if they could give me something so that he could always find me and I agreed, thinking that I was going to get something very cool to play with. He explained otherwise and showed it to me. It was so tiny that you could hardly see it. Then he said it would go here pointing to the back of his neck not realizing until it was to late that his bony hands were showing again.

Something was placed beside me on the table, which I slowly tried to slide into my pocket. However, something grabbed it and slowly pulled it back out. Then he said that they were going to place something over my head and to be very still. I could not see it but it made my skull feel like Jello and I could feel it coming apart. That's the best of my recollection. In a while, everything seemed all right again and he asked me to stand back where I first arrived. He said that he had to go now and not to tell anyone about this. I agreed and heard a loud noise like before I placed my hands over my ears and in that moment, I was standing back on the path by the hedges. Everything was fine except that I could not remember how to get home or exactly where I was.

The memory of all the paths I had traveled was gone. I had absolutely no clue as how to get home or where home might be.

That's when I spotted the old man; I walked up to him thinking he might know where I live and how to get there. Old people are like that they always know everything. They always seem to know what everyone is doing. I was right he told me where to go and what direction to turn, as I would get to a certain spot. At that time, I did not understand left and right. Frankly, it still does not make to much sense even to day. From what I gather and half the population agrees with me; and the other half thinks they have it down pat. Anyway, I started to walk and after a few turns I could see the hotel. By the time I got there my memory had come back, everything was back to normal, and my normal routine, find food and have a nap. There wasn't any discomfort in neither my neck nor my back but my neck was a little itchy and still is to day at times.

I looked at Sally and Ed. It seemed that they were rather speechless. Shit happens but if you close your eyes then sometimes it gets bigger, I thought to myself.

"Well! Do you want me to continue or what"? I asked.

"O' ya answered Ed you just caught me of guard, I've read some books on abductions I just wasn't expecting that.

"I was just trying to figure out what they were doing to you" Answered Sally.

I just shrugged my shoulders and sat there.

"Is there more of that and is that the whole story" Asked Ed.

"Ya, there is more of that but that's not the whole story" I said.

"Ya don't want to answer any questions at all about it," Asked Sally

"What's your question?" I asked.

Did anything change after that, like was there something different about you? Asked Sally

"I can answer that I responded; but I wouldn't mind having something to drink first.

"What can I get you, asked Ed more hot chocolate"?

"No something cold, got any root beer"?
"You bet, root beer coming up" Answered Ed

A Small Voice

A Small Voice
Is
Like the wind, that guides our sails across the water

The strength of that voice, our ability to hear it

Will guide us across the waves of the storm that
rides within our souls

With this, our dreams will become our reality

—Roberta Joehle

5

After Ed gave me some root beer and I lit another cigarette slowly watching those smoke curls that I love so much I continued with Sally's question.

Two things did change after I had been picked up. One was my strength-increased dramatically. Anywhere in the range of two to three times the normal strength; although I can't see any reason for this being done nor any purpose in it, it did become useful to me in a few ways but not that beneficial for my body. I really think that it was either a side affect or an experiment. Over the years, I forgot about it but back when it first happened it came in very handy.

I had found an old wooden boat that had been left abandoned in a dry riverbed. To me it was a dream come true. My very own boat, I could see it had cracks in it and would sink fast if it was in the water. However, that was not the only problem. It was a long way from the lake and I would need to get it over a 15-foot high dam before hitting the water. The boat was also very heavy. It was the same as the boats that they would rent at the lake. Usually it took two big farm boys to drag them back to the boathouses. It was just a matter of what I wanted, not what was possible or not. First, I went to see the rental guys and asked them how to fix a boat like theirs. They told me to use some tar and even gave me some old can that had a little in the bottom. I knew what they were up to. They thought that I would get the stuff all over me and they thought that would be funny. I suppose it came to that but they never saw it, so there! The project of fixing this boat and launching it in the lake took about 3 days. The last day was the longest. After patching it all up and then covering the tar with paper so as not to get anymore on me, I proceeded with the plan of sliding it to the dam. This did not take that long but getting it over the dam was something else. I gathered up ropes and sticks to begin the lifting, pushing the boat up and tightening the rope over and over until I had it over the dame. I can guarantee you that this would have normally been impossible for someone my age and weight. Regardless believe what you will. Once it was over the dam, it was just a matter of getting it across and over a sort railing. By the time, I got it in the water it was already getting dark. It seemed to be leaking a bit so before lunching my very first boat I would need something to bail with. At that time, I could not swim and did not want to take the chance of it filling with water.

"O' no not again" Interrupted Sally laughing and shaking her head.

"You just don't get it that's what life is all about" I answered shaking my head as if she was the one that was crazy.

"Anyway" I said, my plan was to get the boat back to a place where very few people ever went. I felt that would be a good place to hide it. Just a matter of getting across the lake, I could already see the question on Sally's face so I answered it.

"IT'S A BIG LAKE"! I said smiling and continued, by the time I shoved off it was getting very late, my best guess would be midnight. I know that because I was about a 100 feet from shore taking in a fair bit of water when I saw my half brother come barreling to the shore with his bike. What a baby. He was yelling at me and waving his hands. Screaming like a lunatic that I should get back here right now. What a goof I had plans of my own, I proceeded to paddle faster. Paddling, bailing paddling bailing, it has a nice ring to it. I could not believe my eyes; he jumped in the water and began swimming for me. Tossing the bailing can, I paddled like never before while yelling at him to get lost. It wasn't exactly warm out and neither was the water. I discovered for myself just how cold it was when he caught up to me and literally yanked me out of the boat into the water. I couldn't swim and must have taken in a fair bit of water by the time we hit shore. The only thing I remember was him making me run home while he was yelling at me. The next morning I was out before anyone could get a hold of me. But my boat was gone. Over the next few days, I scrounged up some money and rented a small boat. I found it, twenty feet under water. I tried hooks and ropes and it almost capsized the boat I was in, I wanted to get it back to shore but to no avail. Now that I am over forty I realize that I have dreamt of having a sailboat but have never gone for it. Some things really stick with ya. However, this coming summer we are going to change all that. Now it's just a matter of convincing my wife that I am a born sailor and as safe to sail with as possible. I'm thinking of leaving this story out just to make it a little easier. What do you think Sally". I asked

"That might be a good idea" answered Sally laughing

We spent a few minutes talking back and forth regarding my not being necessarily the easiest child to raise. I disagreed after all I was just fine if everyone just would leave me alone.

How Do I Know What's Right for Me?

If I allowed myself to eat all the ice cream, I desired
Would I then crave peas?

If our reality is created by our thoughts and beliefs!

Why do we punish ourselves by creating nasty side
effects?
To something
As wonderful and loving as ice cream?

And why and who made crappy peas good for ya

6

My mother died not long after that incident of the short cut home. Other than school, cutting into my freedom not much changed until the summer of turning nine. Just before school would have ended, I was unwillingly involved in a fight at school. It was lunchtime and all the kids were playing in the front schoolyard. I was at the back entertaining myself as usual when some kids decided to gang up to beat me up. There were about eight of them and one leader they had me cornered. Their self-proclaimed leader was moving forward and the small mark in the back of my neck began to tingle and got very itchy. In a few seconds everything changed, I knew exactly what to do. Take out the leader and the rest will fall, the leader jumped forward to grab me I moved sideways and grabbed him, two seconds later he was laying on the cement out cold. Even though he was bigger than me I had turned him upside down and hammered him into the cement head first, the other kids took off in a hurry.

It was my word against theirs. Not long after that, I was told that I would be going to Canada to live with my aunt and uncle. I did not understand what Canada was nor where it was but I wasn't concerned, because I thought I could always take the train home. In Europe, you can take the train almost to every town you want. People told me that in Canada there where Indians and cowboys like the Wild West I had seen on TV. I was not too impressed by that but I figured it would be an adventure.

My dad had taken me to a big office building to fill out some papers and get my passport. I remember him getting mad at me for not knowing how to spell my name. My first name I could spell but not my last. Later we went to get a suit for me, the one they had picked out did not have any pockets on the inside. I had a plan and I needed pockets, lots and lots of pockets. After making a big enough of a fuss I got my pockets lots of them. Sometimes you gotta stand for what you want and settle for no less.

The plane trip to Canada was very long and uneventful except a trip to the cockpit the man in charge would not let me fly the plan so I wondered why he was wasting my time showing it to me. All it is a tiny room filled with buttons that your not allowed to touch. What fun is that?

Sally was rubbing her for head again. I was going to ask if she was getting a headache, I let it go and continued.

Drank lots of pop and went to the bathroom a million times. The toilet was the most interesting thing on the plane. I would flush it and run to the window because some man said that I could see it going out if I was really fast. I did not believe him but it was worth trying anyway. I had come to the conclusion long ago that people did not always know the difference of what they know or did not know. Many times people think they know something and they don't. Many times people think they don't know something and they do but don't realize it. I had noticed that people's thoughts and words do not even come close to being the same. Obviously, I now fit into that category to. However, I didn't at that time. I either said nothing or said what I was thinking. I kept this up well past my 30's before I came to realize it was best for me to just shut up. Anyway, I am rambling.

Arrival time came at last and so did customs. The man asked me something in a language I did not understand. He was laughing but sent me a mental picture of me carrying a big gun, so I began to show him mine. First one gun then another then another then another then a knife and another and another and my blowgun and a billions of caps. From one pocket from another pocket, you get the picture. He was impressed and so were about 50 other people.

I think he told me to put it all back. You see there was no way in hell that I was going to be scalped without a fight. Indians and cowboys is all I knew of Canada and so that is what I expected. I expected chuck wagons and dusty deserts. Well you can imagine my disappointment when all I saw was a city. Vancouver BC, that's where I landed. Rosedale near Chilliwack, BC is where I would spend many years.

"Wow where did you keep all those guns" Asked Ed laughing.

"In my pockets I answered I had lots of pockets".

"You didn't think that a cap gun was going to save you did you" asked Sally shaking here head

"Of course I did if there was going to be shooting how are thy going to know that it's not a real gun, I said sometimes a bark is better then a bite". Besides, they are not ordinary cap guns I redesigned them, silly. Takes a long time to stick those caps together but you get one big bang and a lot of smoke. Your just like my wife you just don't understand the big bang theory. No, bang no interest. I tried to tell my wife the story of when I got my fire truck, but she didn't see my point at all.

"O" so you think the women don't understand your big bang theory," responded Sally

Ed was being remarkably silent which is what I should have been. Sometimes you are cornered and there is a chance of getting out and other times its best to accept that you're going down in flames. This was looking like one of those times.

Well some can and some can't. I said squirming hoping I could figure a way out of this corner. It is like this, there was a girl that was the daughter of another hotel owner and she use to come around and always wanted to play with me but I didn't like her.

"O" so you could have had friends you just did not what them to be girls now I see" Interrupted Sally.

"No No that's not it I said, it's just that she was a tattle tale. Once I got this fire truck that squirted water out of a hose on the ladder. I had this truck in my fort under some concrete stairs. The stairs where closed off except a tiny hole which I could fit thru. She wanted to know where my fire truck was and I said that I would show her if she promised not to tell anyone, she agreed. So, I showed her my fort and by the way, what good is a water squirting fire truck without fire. So, I lit a small candle to show her how well the truck works. I barely had the candle out when she shoots out of the fort and went straight to my dad. Of course, that was the end of my fire truck, never saw it again and the fort was sealed off. So there, a promise is a promise is a promise.

"You could have been hurt" Said Sally.

Ya I could have been lost in the woods and starved, could have had the plane go down and crash, could have been kidnapped held for ransom and cut to pieces, could have died of loneliness or broken heart from broken promises. We seem bet on protecting everyone from the possible but seem to miss what is already happening.

"I think that you're right Sally; interrupted Ed but there is a story in the story that Klaus is telling".

I think I should go home this is all coming out wrong. How much do I owe for the bill? I asked standing up.

Sally jumped off her stool and said, "I didn't mean to upset you"!

"No it came out all wrong," I answered I just realized what was bugging me about that all these years. I do not know why I did not see it before.

I sat back down and thought about it for a few minute. We all sat in silence while I contemplated my new old forgotten decision.

"Can I get you anything? asked Sally I feel kind of bad".

No, you said what was on your mind and it was the perfect thing to say. "Maybe I will have another hot chocolate with some whip cream just to ease the pain," I said smiling.

I got up and paced back and forth for a bit. Shaking my head, I said that I could not believe that I missed this all this time, Unbelievable!

"I could see how you might be upset at women; you have carried this with you for a long time and projected it forward" Added Ed while I was pacing.

"No that's not it," I answered still pacing I had a similar thing happen a few years later with a boy. I don't care about that I was upset at losing the fire truck and my fort and I was upset at her but not for what she did but why she did it. It was not her either she was just the straw that had broke the camels back.

"Sally came back with the hot chocolate while adding some whip cream she said. I heard what you said but there is question still burning in my mind. I hope you don't mind me asking".

Ed spoke up laughing, "That's my Sally always saying what's on her mind no matter what".

Stick with it its working even if it doesn't seem that way sometimes" I answered, what's the question?

What happened to that boy, did he die"?

"No the kid who started the trouble did not die. He just spent a week in the hospital and a few more weeks in bed at home. I went to see him to apologize. His parents left the room for a minute and that is when he apologized to me. I don't think that I ever saw him after that" I answered.

"So what's up with the fire truck thing" Asked Sally.

Approval I said that is what it was all about getting love thru approval. She did not want me to get into trouble she needed love and the only way she knew how to get it was by getting approval for her actions. You have to remember that I heard people's thoughts so I knew what was going on and I had seen that many times in everybody. Almost everyone's thoughts are based on getting approval and by that getting love. Even trying to be successful at something seemed to be based on approval. Think about it we all want to be successful at what we do but how much is based on approval to get love. Really think about it how many of our actions, decisions, words and the things we do are based on getting approval in some way and by that getting a feeling of love. If you need love bad enough and by that approval then it becomes hard, to tell the difference between what we really want to do and what is about approval. You see I said, sitting down now. I had decided never to do anything for approval and only that which was right for me. I know what your thinking Sally a child does not necessarily have the life experience to know exactly always what is right for them but that's a learning experience no more dangerous then doing things for approval and love.

This has caused so much grief in my life and why I was missing so much love. I wasn't getting approval from people for what I was doing so I was not getting any love either. The problem is that there needs to be a balance and I went to the opposite end. I'm not sorry for that I just did not understand it all until today. Do you see what I mean?

"More then I want to answered Ed more than I want to"…

I agree answered Sally I'll have to give that some more thought".

Me too I responded anyway do you want to hear the rest".

"Definitely" answered Ed. "Definitely" answered Sally.

OK then lets leave this for some other time of contemplation.

Perceptions

A student walking along with his master teacher
Saw a green stick lying on the ground and asked his
master teacher
What is color?
At that moment the master picked up the stick and
said
Green is the color you will hate and fear
Then he struck him many times
As he laid the stick down, he said
That is how your perceptions of what is, is colored!
Only Love sees clearly beyond color, words and
action
This color that stick my actions will be like a thorn
that only
Forgiveness of Love can remove
Until then, it will be a burden of sword and shield…
Color is a perception

7

"**I** think that I am going to move forward in time and get all the alien encounters over with before moving on" I said continuing with the story.

My next encounter was just shortly after turning sixteen. I had my driver's license and was just returning from spending time with some friends. That is right I had some friends mostly short term but friends never the less. Anyway ten minutes from home my car started to act up and finally quit running. At the time I was driving an old beetle I got out of the car and was going to open the back hatch when I heard a high pitched sound same as before. Two seconds later I was again in the same ship as before looking at the same elf or alien as before. This took me by surprise for I had come to the conclusion that the first time was just a dream. He greeted me and asked how I was. It took a while but we ended up talking for what seemed a long time. I told him all that had happened and some of the trouble I was having in school not being able to read and write. I cannot honestly remember all that was said but a lot of it only had to do with my life. I even asked if I could go with them. He said that I could not do that yet but maybe some day. I asked to see the ship but he said that we were running out of time and that I could only stay on this ship for only so long before I would lose my balance on my reality. I did not fully understand that. However, I think I do now. He said that they could probably fix my writing and reading part if I want, I said OK. He asked me to sit on the same table as before and two others came in who then stood behind me. Even though I was told to be very still I now could see that certain gadgets were coming from an opening in the ceiling. Something was placed over my scull and I could feel my scull turning soft like jello. He was saying certain things to me that did not totally make sense at the time. He said that it would help but not be perfect for they could only do so much without causing problems with other things that they wanted to stay the same; whatever that meant. He also said that they would be opening something that would mean I would understand some things without learning them and to not to worry, I still trusted him and agreed. However, something went wrong and I could sense the urgency from him and from the two behind me. There was a split second where I could have sworn that I was someone else but then everything went black. The next thing I know I was sitting back in my car but I could not remember who I was. It was as if I was on some alien planet everything looked strange. This is hard to explain. I still remembered everything but not as mine, it was as if I had stepped into someone else's life. You might relate this to what some call walk-ins but I don't think so. The rest of the story later might be a clue. You see in our minds and in our DNA lies all we have ever done and known in this life and others past and probable. However, you want to see it. I think that something had opened to far when they were working on me and I think they either were not able to close it all the way or were trying to keep it open a certain amount. That is why I can now write and speak in several different languages that are not recorded in our history. However, not in English?

"I'm not sure if I get what you are trying to say" interrupted Ed.

"Well that makes two of us," I said laughing. What I am trying to say is that what we try to learn is already there in our minds as we think we are learning something it is just slowly being released which gives us the appearance that we are learning it, when in fact we already have it. I think you will see what I mean; there is a theory that I agree with and it is that all the knowledge that we have learnt over our lifetimes if stored in our DNA like a program in a computer. Our minds are there to access this information if we know how, Se what I mean.

"Sort of I guess," answered Ed.

OK so over the next, few weeks' things balanced out but my spelling did not improve one bit. On the other hand, I could read fluently and became so obsessed with my new talent that I skipped so many classes that the teachers knew where to find me. I was in the library reading everything. You could usually find me in behind a stack of books reading two or three at once. Most of the teachers seemed content to leave me there. Sometimes they asked a few questions about what I was reading and seemed satisfied enough with the answers to leave me there. So there, you go make of it what you want. One day I cannot read and a few days later, I can. It was not long before I began reading anything I could get my hands on as far as metaphysical stuff, out of body travel, science and so on. I should tell you that I do not totally read as you do I see pictures. The words form pictures. I may read about atoms but I see different pictures than what is written or drawn. Science has a long way to go, what I call the underground science has understanding of things that the public scientists have no clue of even being possible. Anyway, I had better stop with that this is not what this story is about so we will move along.

"Wait a minute what about what you call the underground science." Asked Ed leaning forward.

"I cannot get into that it will take us way of base," I answered.

Ed would not leave it alone. Therefore, we probably spent the next half an hour discussing various aspects of what some call the underground science. I'm not going to get into that in this book because my purpose is to discover the power behind love not the conspiracy theory. There are many books on the market that will give you much to think about. If you want proof all you need to do is learn to either travel out of your body or if that scares you then learn to remote view. I'd say have fun but that is not a discovery that you are going to like.

Besides, until you learn about sending love there will be nothing you can do about it. So, my suggestion is that you first become a master at sending love. Do, as you will.

IF this is not your planet,
Then get lost!!!

8

OK so only two more to go are you ready I asked before continuing.

The next and second last time I had a visited was years later. By that time, I was married and had a son. I owned and operated a small dairy farm just south of Spedden Alberta.

It was very late at night I had to get up and go to the barn to check on a pregnant cow that was ready to give birth. After getting to the barn and checking on the cow I pushed some hay up that the other cows had pushed back trying to get at the best stuff first.

I was very depressed in those days. I loved my cows and enjoyed farming but at the same time, I felt like I was wasting my life away. I had different plans at one time of writing out theories, ideas and things that I had come to understand; but due to my inability to right had lost my confidence. Also, it seemed that no one believed in even the simplest things I discovered. As an example, if you look at some farms you will notice that most of the wooden fences have been chewed on. This is not because of a need to chew, but because the animals are missing certain forms of minerals. It took a while to figure out what they were and in what form they need to be, but never the less I figured it out. The people at the animal research station were not interested even though they had come to my farm several times to try to figure out what I was doing. My cows were producing large amounts of milk and not loosing any weight. This was because of the food intake. After they had weighed and measured what my cows were eating in order to gain weight instead of loosing it they decided that it was impossible for them to eat that much and that it was just a fluke. They said that in all the tests that they have done there was a limit on what a cow could consume for a given weight. They just kept going over things looking for mistakes instead of listening to what I was trying to explain to them. I tried to explain it to them but it went over their heads. Too much education in the wrong direction, they could not deny what was happening they just could not explain it and did not want my explanation. It still baffles me today how narrow-minded people can become. They did send other dairy farmers who had production problems to me. However, they did not get it either. It is so simple. I realized I was getting off track and continued with the story.

After pushing the hay forward, I was sitting on a bale of hay thinking about exactly what I just mentioned. I guess in some way I was lonely and wanted to be in the company of like-minded people.

I heard that high-pitched sound and knew exactly what was coming. I was instantly on the ship. Only this time I was already sitting on the table. This was not to be a pleasant visit as I had hoped. There were three behind me now instead of two. The other one standing in front of me seemed very agitated and in a hurry, he said that it was almost time for me and that we would need to do some more changing. I tried to ask what, where, when and why but it had already begun. I went in and out of consciousness several times and in-between those times I would hear them say that there was something happening with the ship or they were under attack. I was picking up bits and pieces of mental conversations that did not make a lot of sense. However, something was going wrong. My landing was not very smooth either. Instead of being placed back, where they had picked me up I found myself in mid air falling into a pile of manure. It wasn't even all that soft of a landing. I did not see any ship but I did hear what sounded like thunder in a clear sky. After going, back to the house and getting cleaned up. I had something to eat. Then I headed back to the barn. This time I was getting very annoyed and decided that the next time would be different. Next time I am getting some answers I said to myself. As it turned out the next time was not for another ten years. Nevertheless, I didn't forget. Over the years, all of this had taken its toll on me. I had also learned some tricks of my own. We'll get into that later. I figured it was only a matter of time before I received an opportunity to try out my newfound abilities.

"I think I need a cigarette; all this is bringing back a lot of memories", I said lighting a smoke.

"So the guys from the research center were just coming out to your farm because your cows were fat", asked Sally laughing. "Hey Ed Klaus has fat cows".

"Very funny, they were fat cows"! The thing is they were producing large amounts of milk. Cows can produce 10 gallons and more a day. That causes them to loose a lot of weight. The problem is that they can't eat enough food to supply them with what they need and so they start to lose weight. At some point, they will slow down milk production because they are just worn out. Therefore, the research people work on ways to change protein so that it can be absorbed faster. This and other things do help but do not solve the problem. And you can't exactly turn the milk off. So one night we had some guests we had mashed potatoes and roast everyone ate until we where stuffed. I couldn't eat one more bite of potatoes I was that stuffed. As it turned out we had desert and they had brought desert also. The fact is that even though I was so stuffed that I could not eat one bite of potatoes I was able to eat two desserts and coffee. That's when it hit me. Three to five course meals. See even when you're stuffed of one thing you can always find room for something else. That was the trick. I gave my cows a four-course meal in the morning, a three-course meal at noon and five-course meal at night. The result was that they where able to eat 30% more food than what was statistically proven to be the maximum per body weight. Simple…my cows gained weight and produced large amounts of milk for long periods of time. What they could not understand or did not want to acknowledge was that a cow is just like us when it comes to food. The bottom line was that they said that what my cows where eating was impossible and that was that. Anyway, the fence-chewing thing went much the same way. It took a long time to figure out what minerals they were missing but in the end I was told that cows do not need those minerals, "Whatever"! I told them.

Anyway, it seems I got of track again; the problem was that after I was picked up things went all to hell. For the next two years, I could hear people's thoughts but not their conscious thoughts their unconscious thoughts. This almost drove me insane. I ended up leaving the marriage and the farm.

"Well what happened to the farm", Asked Ed

"I signed it over to my wife," I answered.

"I don't fully get what happened" Asked Sally

Everything just took its toll on me and that is all there is to it. Besides, by that time I had decided that I was just nuts. There is no cure for insanity.

"That's what you believed, that you where insane," observed Sally

"Well you take what I explained so far and add a hundred more tiny things not worth mentioning individually and you have insanity," I answered. One poke in the arm is nothing, but a hundred add up to more than a hefty punch. That's the way it went and that is the way I began to see it. There is more and more and more. Anyway talking about it is one thing living it day to day is another. Coming to Canada and living with my aunt and uncle was like going to hell. I don't want to go into the details, but what happened there and my inability to write ended up crushing every bit of self-esteem. Children and people can be very resilient through things that happen but if your self-esteem is crushed your finished. Once you can build up self-esteem then anything becomes possible. Obviously, I wrote a book even though I can't write but I had to rebuild my self-esteem first. This took a long time, a very long time.

"I can understand that," said Sally

"Did they come back again," Asked Ed

"Ya one more time so far," I answered. It was late fall 1998 more than 10 years later, but at the same time as I was starting to get some good results from my lottery experiment and just started learning about sending love. You have read my first book so you know what time I am talking about.

"That's when Sneaky first came onto the scene," Responded Sally

"Ya I think I know when you mean, Interrupted Ed, except that story was a lot funnier then this one. I'm not complaining now waving his hand, it's just that I expected something different".

"Me too" answered Sally.

I shrugged my shoulders saying I didn't make the path I just slid down it. you don't need to hear it. I could see that they were having a hard time swallowing this story. I don't blame them. They wanted to believe. It's a good thing that the burden of proof lies with the disbeliever not with the storyteller.

"There is no proof Sally, Ed. I said, even if you had lived it even then it still would not prove itself to you". That's just the way it is.

"If I had been there then that would be proof to me" Answered Sally

"No it wouldn't I answered back it would seem like a dream". Its like a hit and run and after its hard to tell who hit and who ran. Besides there is something your not aware of the time deferential on those ships is different. Its very confusing to the conscious mind and so it tries to write it off as a dream.

"What do you mean by time being different" Asked Ed

I think it would be better if I finish this part of the story first then we can go into discussing time that way it wont get to confusing.

Everybody agreed so I continued.

It was About 8 or 9 pm at night I suddenly felt very tired. Feeling that I couldn't hold my eyes open for another minute went to my bedroom and laid on the bed. I'm sure I was out as soon as I hit the bed. Where I woke up was a different story. With all the deep and long meditations I was doing at that time, I had trained myself to wake up at the first sign of any danger. In other words, I had instructed my subconscious to wake me fully at any sign of trouble. This came in very handy, because I woke up on another ship. I woke up very fast with my adrenalin already pumping. With what I saw I made an instant decision that I was not somewhere friendly and not with someone friendly. Sitting up instantly, I must have scared the heck out of the three aliens. It definitely looked like they were about to do something to my head. One of them very forcefully said to me to lie down so they can continue. Not much chance of that, I grabbed him by the neck a very small neck at that. My hand went all the way around, He tried with his little fingers to get my grip off but after many years of dairy farming, I have a steel grip. One of the others came around the table to help but I had him the same way. The struggle only lasted seconds before I felt the first neck snap. He dropped like a rag doll. The other I punched in the head and let go of his neck at the same time, he flu of his feet and hit the back wall. When I punched him in the head, I could feel his scull crushing under my fist. The third one made it to a door or better said an opening in the wall. I jumped off the table to grab him but missed and tripped. That was his saving grace. Getting up I ran after him but felt heavy and slowed by my weight. There were two others coming down the hallway as he passed them I felt something hit me. For a second it froze my body and I fell. While getting back up, I saw that one of the two others had some sort of device in his hand. I decided that's who was next but just before reaching him I was hit again, and out cold just long enough to be pushed in a room and have the door closed behind me. I know it was just minutes because I was not totally out of it just rather stunned. The room had many people in it probably anywhere from 10 to 15. All of them seemed out of it and either lying on the floor or on the floor leaning against a wall. One was standing. I got up and rushed over to him. He seemed oblivious to what was happening. I was mad and would have killed every one of those little bastards if given the chance. I started slapping the one who was standing and yelling at him to wake up and fight. There was no reaching him at all. I ran to several other people slapping and kicking them trying to get them to become conscious and fight but they where out of it. Some were dressed and others looked like they had been taken from there beds. I did everything I could to try to wake them up but to no avail. I started shaking the one that was standing again, thinking he was my best chance when it seemed like there was an explosion somewhere on the ship. It was loud and shook the whole ship. Two seconds later there was another. I ran to the door and tried to open it by fidgeting with the symbols on the side of the door. The next second I was in another room of a ship; somehow I was transported to the ones that had picked me up before. This time I was standing in the main control room with what ever his name might be. There were others sitting at control panels. The whole front of the ship was invisible you could see out as if it was wide open. This made me very dizzy as it felt like I could have fallen out. I braced myself on some kind of panel and watched. It seems the ship I had come from had a whole chunk ripped out of it. All of this was happening very fast. I got the impression that they were trying to get others out of the damaged ship but were having some trouble. It was all over in a matter of seconds. There was another ship approaching and it had already fired two shots at the damaged ship. The ship exploded and then there was nothing left…

We seemed to turn and move away from the other ship. The whole wall where you could see out of the ship turned solid. I was so mad it felt like I was breathing fire. I made myself very clear, I want to go home and be put exactly where I was found and I never want to see you again. OK so I might have said a few more things before sitting down on the floor and leaning against a wall. The only thing that was said to me was that they would think you are dead in this time line and will attempt to go after you in another time line. To be honest I was not listening I was extremely mad. My anger was mostly covering up my feelings of helplessness because I have no weapons and no ship nothing to fight with and don't even know who the good guys are or who the bad guys are or how the hell I got involved with this. It would all become clear to me with in two years.

A few days later, I asked sneaky about this but he was not very forthcoming. All he said was that there are two forces in the universe. One will stop you and the other will drive you forward the trick is to use them both to drive you to your goals and beyond.

Frankly, I am not sure what all this was about nor what the purpose was. The only thing that has come from it is some centers of my mind are open that perhaps should not have been. Regardless personally my opinion is that I could have done a better job at this without all this interference.

"So what do you think?" I asked Sally and ed.

"Wow that's something else," answered Ed shaking his head

"So what happened to the people on that ship that was blown up" Asked Sally

"Dead, I would think, I answered there was no indication that they were taken over to the other ship".

"Did you ask" Asked Sally

"No I didn't ask anything at all But I could tell that things had not gone as planned. Or maybe they had but they wanted it to look like it failed".

I" wonder why responded Sally This is all very confusing, will you be writing this in your next book she asked".

"Actually, I was thinking of writing it out just as I am telling you it now" I answered.

"Do you mean that we will be in the book like Nena and Danny?" Asked Sally

"That is the idea so does everything make sense so far".

"Ya I think if you write it as you have explained it so far it is understandable" responded Ed but I would think that it would raise many questions. I know I have a lot of them now I just did not want to interrupt you while you were telling your story. Like why would they go after you like that"?

Well I had some information that I did not realize I had until later its all connected to sending love. I'll tell you what it is later and when I do you will say that you knew it you just seemed to have forgotten it.

What do you think would happen if an entire race of billions of people worked from their power source? Just think about the implications, but there is another piece to all of this.

"How do you feel about what you did to those aliens? Don't you think that there might be some retaliation?" Asked Sally

"I don't think so I think that they were very busy and probably have their hands full and I think that they think I'm dead. As far as how I feel about it, I do not know, mixed feelings I guess."

"From reading your last book I did not think you would have that in you I don't want to upset you but it seems from what you told us that you where almost doing more then protecting yourself. Its almost like revenge, is there something you're not telling us? Asked Sally".

Ed was starring at me with anticipation.

I sat silent trying to think of what I should say.

"Are you going to be leaving things out in this book too asked Ed grinning"?

I stopped talking as some people were coming into the restaurant. They were going back and forth not able to decide if they should stay or not. Finally, they sat down, but seemed nervous. Sally gave them a minute and then went to see what they would like.

Everything is a path that leads to other paths, I answered I think its best to finish the rest of the story as a whole and then maybe look down some of the other possibilities and of how all of it might be connecting. This sending love thing is the connection. That is one of the reasons why I want to write this book. To try to explain in some way that sending love can have such an impact on people and the planet as a whole that I believe some will and are truing to stop it and some are trying to bring it about and some want it to happen but in a controlled way.

What do you mean by that some want it to happen but in a controlled way? Asked Ed

"They want to control it for there own purposes" I answered, as more and more people start to send love the planet will start to be filled with love and then also begin radiating love outward that will have ramifications that go beyond this solar system affecting everyone and everything just like the sun does. The sun is radiating light we will be radiating love.

Unless your vibrating with love you won't be able to come hear anymore then you would be able to land on the sun. It also means that a lot of civilization would need to change or move. I say this loosely and in physical terms, but it makes the point".

Did I miss anything; asked Sally they only wanted coffee".

"O' good" answered Ed

So what did I miss"? Asked Sally again.

While you explain it Ed and I will take a bathroom break" I answered getting up

By the time I came back from the washroom the people were already getting up to leave and Sally came back and sat down.

"What were you doing in there for so long anyway?" asked Sally laughing.

Was I in there for a long time? It didn't seem that way to me" I answered smiling

"Time must be different for Klaus" answered Ed laughing

"So you think that this sending love is so powerful that it will effect people or aliens on other planets" Asked Sally.

"It appears that way," I answered. I guess it depends what people do with it. It's like this, I get a lot of email from what some call world meditations where a lot of people get together around the world and send a feeling and thoughts of peace like a blanket over the world. Also, a lot of people talk about the power of love but what they are missing is actually sending love and also focusing that love at certain events or people. It's like this if there is a fire and you have a certain amount of water if you spread it all over the place it will just evaporate you focus it to certain places to contain the fire and then when you have it under control you put it out.

Lets say you have a thousand people once a week meditating and sending thoughts of peace all over the world you won't get much of a result but if you train those same people to send love and then focus them on a target you will see results very fast.

"If there is a war and you want to stop it would you not send love to the entire country that is at war;" asked Ed

No you would focus on the leaders of both sides because they have the power to call a seize fire and end the war. By filling them with love, they will make different decisions. And by focusing on them, you are creating what you want to achieve. Then as a seize fire begins you then begin working outwards to the people.

"What about free will asked Ed is it not they're right to do as they want"?

O' good one that's sort of like the sun saying, O' boy maybe I should not shine today because some people will not like it they want darkness so I had better not shine. There is sunlight there is air and water and there is going to be love radiating out. That is the destiny of this planet. Sending love does not stop you from playing war games I myself love those games and feel people should be free to do what brings them joy. Sending love will not turn everyone into love zombies. If it took away my character, I would dump it as fast as I could. If someone is doing, things out of hate and fear it will work to solve that by removing that inner pain and releasing those trapped fears. If someone or a group of people are doing something that they really enjoy you will be supporting them in that endeavor regardless of what it is even if it could kill them that is there choice and it is there freedom. By you sending them love you are in a sense giving them strength, health, endurance, energy helping them to fulfill what truly brings them joy even if it is not to your liking. Some people think that sending love to someone that did not ask for it is an evasion of privacy. If that's what you, want to believe that's fine with me. I'm going to do what I think is right and since I am the one using my source of power I'll decide my destiny and how my life will be experienced by me. If you are sending love and for some reason it is not right you will know right a way. I have had that happen only once, you can debate it all you want. You have free will to rage war and I have free will to stop it.

"You had mentioned something in the beginning of your last book about Tibet" Mentioned Sally.

"Perfect example" I answered

"O' ya you were saying that if the people of Tibet would have had the knowledge about sending love and did it they could have stopped the invasion" Responded Ed

"Exactly I answered have you ever really thought about that invasion and what it was about?

Think about what is there do you think that there are enough resources there to even pay for the holding army. The point is simple before the invasion there was thousands of monks chanting, praying, and turning their prayer wheels while the leader runs away. If you want to lead people then be prepared to stand with them and die with them. That I can respect and the people of the world would also have respected it and even stood up and joined with them, I'll just stop there before…

Live what you preach and stand with it to the end.

"I hate to say this but are you living what you say? Asked Sally You are rich you don't need to work to make money and so on".

Hold on there what made you think that I am rich," I asked shocked at what she asked

Well you made a lot of money with the lottery and so you do not need to worry how to make a living. I would have lots of time to send love if I did not have to work for a living.

O' I see what your saying. I am not rich I stopped working with the lottery and went to work with sending love and made my living not from the lottery nor from selling the book. I decided that to live what I believed and I have been giving the book away and paying for it. Putting the book out cost me thousands of dollars and none of it came from the lottery. I worked for it and sent love to such a point that I had increased my income considerably so that I needed to only work a fraction of the time. I did this all by sending love by doing exactly what I said in my book. Everything I have is from the result of my sending love. Down the road, there will be some income from the books but that will be then and will still be a result of my sending love.

"O' I did not realize that" answered Sally shyly

All I did was send love and then follow the doors that opened and things just got better and better all the old problems seemed to slowly go away bit by bit. I can tell you a little about that letter but I would like to get this story over with.

"OK that sounds good to me," answered Sally.

Privacy

I read something today about privacy, which made
me laugh

Because there really is no such thing, it's nothing
more than an Illusion

We pick our noses when we think no one is looking
but that's not the case

Life can be hard and it can be fun but nevertheless

It is precious especially life on this planet at this
time

Not everyone can actually come here and there is a
tremendous lineup

Of souls wanting to experience life on earth

In other words to be here especially at this time is
an honor

Which brings me back to privacy because for every
person here

There is at least half a dozen watching us all the
time

Learning and growing from our experiences

Some can't come here and others just prefer to learn
by watching

Which by the way throws privacy right out the
window and the next time you're picking your nose
or doing something you think no one will know
about

Think again

9

We took a short break because the phone had rung and Sally was on it for a few minutes. After she got of the phone, I continued.

OK So we will go back in time for a bit here, back to after I had left the farm and was living in Edmonton. Sometime during the mid 1980 s at that time, I was working for a lumber store. Two main things happened during that time that I had to leave out of the last book. Even though both things were happening at the same time, they are related but the only way I can explain them is to separate them a bit. After I explain it, you can imagine what it was like for me to live thru these things and hold down a regular job. Frankly, I am surprised that I'm still sane enough to write about it. "OK so maybe that's still up for debate" I said laughing but I wasn't laughing on the inside. Let me remind you what you believe and what you don't believe is up to you. An old sorcerer taught me to leave the burden of proof with the disbeliever.

"Works for me" answered Sally. "Works for me" answered Ed

If you haven't read the first book, I'll rewrite some of what started it all. Then continue the story with Sally and Ed as they had read the first book not long before I had arrived at the gas station restaurant. Also, Sally and Ed are no longer there the gas station still is. It's about ¾ of the way from Calgary to Heart Creek and now has a go-cart track there. It's on the south side of the highway. Just in case you want to know.

I had spent several months reading a few books and trying to make a very serious attempt at being happy. I had put a lot of effort in it, but had zero results. I felt like it was getting worse rather than better, and the straw that finally broke the camel's back came one night when I was reading a new book I had just picked up earlier that day. In this book, the person who wrote it described meeting some great teacher who taught him various fascinating things. What really upset me was that this person had some magical teacher come to him out of the blue and teach him all he wanted to know, while I have to struggle with my problems on my own. The other part that upset me was that he told about certain interesting things that he learned but did not give the instructions on how to do it. What's the point of telling me these things without giving me instructions? A waste of paper and a waste of my time." "My attitude at that time had bottomed out a bit." I remember it all, really clearly. I felt that the universe had forgotten about me. I was so frustrated and mad that I threw the book against the wall, and in my mind, I screamed that if I didn't get some help right away, tomorrow morning I was going to take my car to the mountains and drive it over the cliff. I could feel the anger flowing through my veins. In the long run, I probably would not have done it but at that moment in my mind, the decision was made. I figured that as long as I was here the universe could ignore me, but when I'm no longer here and standing in front of it, it's going to be a lot more difficult to ignore me then!"

"I don't know how long it was exactly, but I would say that no more than five minutes after I had screamed those words in my mind, it started. My inner senses just seemed to spring to life and I could feel something very big. It was huge and it seemed to be trying to squeeze itself into my apartment but it was just too big, and ended up taking up space in the entire apartment block, and even that was not enough. I really couldn't see anything, nor hear anything, but I could feel it with my whole being, that's the only way that I can describe it. I cannot tell you how scared I was. I do not think I have ever been that scared. I almost peed my bed."

"I had a small but open apartment, and from my bed I could see the hallway, part of the kitchen, and a large part of my living room, all the lights were on because I don't like the dark. As soon as it gets dark, I have always felt like there is something big standing behind me, watching me. The dark has scared me for as long as I can remember. So I always keep the lights on, I don't even like dark corners, who knows what might be lurking in there? Within a few seconds, the lights started to flash on and off it was not just lights all at once but individual lights in the light tracks I had hanging up. It was almost musical. I was literally shaking with fear. I could feel and sense this presence forming and

all of a sudden, I heard a voice in my head. It said, loudly and firmly,
"You should know better…!"

"And that was it. The lights stopped blinking and whatever it was
left. I was so scared that even though I needed to go to the washroom
really badly, I did not leave my bed until the next morning. Nor did I
sleep in my apartment the next night. The weird part was there was a
strange hush that came over the entire apartment building and stayed
for several weeks. I heard two other people talking in the laundry room
several days later, and apparently other people in the apartment build-
ing had also sensed something, but could not explain what it was."
Now for the part that I left out.

That night was the beginning of getting what I asked for. It took a
couple of weeks to develop but you might say it started slowly and then
went out of control very fast. You know I have tried to think back on
that night and I have tried to remember exactly what I asked for but I
can't exactly remember, I know I had something in my mind but I
can't seem to remember what it was that got me what I got. It became
an on going nightmare that lasted for 12 years or so. I'm going to tell
you this part in one swing no interruptions.

"OK" answered Ed

Sometime in April of, 1987 I woke up early one morning it was a
rough night of many dreams. All I could remember was that there was
some kind of battle going on. All that remained was pieces. I remember
the morning very clearly nothing could ever wipe it from my memory.
I was totally drained and felt like I had just battled my life away. I
remember slowly getting out of bed in order to get ready to go to work
but as I slipped out of bed, I felt very strange, sort of, as if I was out of
my body or perhaps I could say seemingly separated from my body.
Feeling dizzy and disoriented, I decided to lie down again for ten minutes or so before getting ready for work.

Before closing my eyes, I noticed that everything seemed rather gray
and pale. I must have drifted off to sleep rather quickly because the
next thing that transpired to my knowledge is that I seemed to be
standing in someone else's body. He was carrying some sticks of wood

in his arms. In some way, it almost felt as if I was carrying these pieces of wood in my arms but I could tell it was not my body and I wasn't in control of it. Yet, at the same time it felt like he was me. The best way to explain this strange phenomenon is that two of us were in the same body having all the feelings and sensation that go with it, except that he had control. He/we, we're going along picking up more pieces of wood, sometimes stopping for a moment to split or shorten some pieces with a make shift axe that could be described as medieval. Everything was as real as every day life and extremely confusing because I could hear his thoughts as mine to the point that I could hardly tell that they were his thoughts. Some thoughts I knew were not mine because of what he was thinking. He was married and according to his thoughts, he was married to the most beautiful woman in his world. He was also very happy. I wasn't married and neither was I all that happy. I tried to look around but I couldn't turn my head nor move my eyes anywhere other than what he was looking at. What I did see was rolling hills with patches of trees scattered here and there. Many trees had already lost their leaves and there was a definite fragrance of fall in the air. I knew this wasn't real and just a dream. It was as if I was dreaming but fully conscious of the fact that I was dreaming. It was also more real than any dream I ever had. I'm not sure why I did not panic all things considered I should have. I think it was him, he was at peace and happy in a very simple way. In some way his feelings became mine or perhaps I just accept them as mine.

His hands and arms their very tanned they looked like they had done hard work. His hands and arms were very much like mine except perhaps shorter, or at least so it seemed. It was a very odd feeling to have hands doing things without my thoughts connected to them yet I was seeing them through his eyes as if they should have been mine. He was picking up dry branches that had fallen from the trees. I kept seeing the ground moving closer and a hand reaching for a stick and putting it on top of the pile that the other hand was holding. I could hear his thoughts as if they were mine. Pick, find more wood and head home for breakfast. Not the word breakfast just an early morning meal. A small piece of wood or sliver was caught in-between two fingers, I could feel it but at the same time, I couldn't react.

I tried to close my eyes or his eyes and will myself home back to my body but I couldn't close my eyes other than when he linked. Normally I don't pay any attention to when I blink but in this case, I was not in control, which made it as obvious as having someone turning the lights on and off. Just when I would see or spot something through his eyes he would blink or rub his eyes, this was getting a little annoying and every time I try to will myself home to my body he would decide that it was time to go home but then at the last minute he would spot another piece of wood.

What was taking up most of my time was that our thoughts where mixing. If I thought something then he would think it in his own terms and then I would think it again as it if our thoughts where going around in circles. He was also feeling a little out of place even though he didn't have the words to describe it. Which I suppose is to be expected considering I was also in his body. I wasn't nervous or scared but I did have a bad feeling.

All of a sudden, there was a shiver that went up his spine, as he turned two pieces of wood fell from the pile he had in his arm. He was looking over a hill and seemed certain to be expecting to see smoke. Apparently, he had lit the fire before going to get more wood. It was a very chilly morning and he felt that his wife and son would have kept the fire going. He had more firewood stored up it was just a regular morning chore to collect more wood on a daily bases. He thought that there definitely should be smoke considering that there was no breeze. Which is something I hadn't noticed.

There was a moment of stillness in his mind, in my mind. In the moments that followed I became nervous of this dream or he became nervous, I'm not sure who started it but he became more alarmed and without picking up the pieces of wood he had dropped moments before, he began to walk towards some hill he was staring at. At that moment, I had no idea what would transpire nor that it would affect the rest of my life. We/he started walking at a slow pace which became slightly quicker with each step. The closer he got to the hill the more determined he was that there should be some smoke visible. By the time we had reached the top of this hill, he had already dropped several more pieces of wood.

It was difficult to focus and to separate his thoughts from mine because he had so many thoughts racing into his mind and at the same time, pushing them away saying everything is fine.

When we reached the top of this hill, I could see a small building mostly made out of what looked like sod with a few beams of wood here and there. There was a small fence built partly out of rocks and branches. There were three horses standing in front of this building which by now I had gathered was his home but they were not his horses. The house was no more than perhaps two hundred yards away, he could clearly see there was no smoke coming from the chimney but it's the horses that made him anxious. Within seconds, he dropped all the wood he was carrying and began to run down the hill. As we were running he was clutching a small makeshift axe in one hand that was tied to his waist, I only got a short glimpse of it. Ten feet before the building he stopped, staring at the door and listening. His heart was racing. He, we only stood there for a few seconds, his heart was beating a mile a minute, thoughts were racing around his mind. I felt num almost sick to my stomach. For some reason the thought of a window came into his mind. I noticed that there were no windows. The house was mostly made of mud and rocks. A few sticks here and there poking out of the straw roof. The whole house was barely the size of a single car garage. Three horses where tied to some rocks lying on the ground.

There was what sounded like a muffled scream, the next thing I knew, he was at the door and was pushing it open very forcefully.

What happened next seemed like it took only seconds but those moments are forever burnt into my mind. Possibly, but not necessarily forgivable, but not forgettable. I became lost in what he saw and what he felt, everything else fell away. At that point, it felt like I was him there was no distinction.

Ed and Sally where at the edge of their seats I stopped for a moment to catch my breath and to get hold of my feelings. Talking about this brought it all back and all the feelings that came with it.

"What happened next is a bit ugly," I said looking at Ed and Sally but here it goes.

As the door flew open what happened and the feelings that went with it was like an emotional explosion.

Also by that time what he knew, I knew we had merged together. His wife was laid on a table, there was someone on top of her and another was holding her down, there was a third man standing a few steps from the table laughing and drinking something. I cannot describe what came up in him as he saw this and I don't think you can imagine it because there is nothing I have ever felt to compare it to. I had not noticed it but he already had the axe in his hand. There was a moment of shock from him and from them but it was in that moment that he reacted 3 steps forward and the axe went into the back of the man that was on top of his wife. There was a scream from him at the same time the man holding her tried to react by going for his knife but he pulled the axe out of that first mans back and swung it with precisian right across the throat of the second man there was a burst of blood. Still holding the axe, he made one circle and threw the axe at the third man hitting him in the chest he fell backwards with the axe stuck in his chest. Then without a thought he untied the one arm of his wife that was tied up and tried to pull her to him. The man on top of her had rolled off on to the floor he picked up his wife into his arms she seemed in very bad shape and hardly aware of what was going on. As he picked her up I think his intentions where to put her on to a small bed in one corner of the room and that's when I felt something in him snap because of what he saw. His son was on the floor with his throat cut. I'll spare you the rest of that by omitting the details of it. His wife died a few hours later in his arms. One of the men was still alive by this time he died later slowly but not before telling me who they were, where they came from and who their families were.

Sometime later, I came out of this dream like state but I was totally exhausted and emotionally drained. It was not like watching a movie because I was him I felt everything and even after I came out of this it felt like I still was him and it felt like it just happened to me at that moment in my life. I don't know how to explain it other than say there was no distinction between his life and mine.

I could see Ed wanted to ask something but did not know what to say tears where rolling down Sally's face.

"I'll explain it to you I said it will make sense at the end".

I stretched a bit and tried to discharge my emotions. Ed just nodded his head; I don't think that Sally wanted to hear much more so I cut it short and left out the gory parts.

So, let me explain it this way over the next 12 years 4 to 5 nights a week in my dreams I would become him and live his life and no matter what I did I could not shut it down. This was exhausting and almost maddening. In his life I was a fish out of water and coming back in the mornings to my life did not feel much better over time I became so use to it that it was just a part of my life I was him. There was a big difference between his life and mine. I smoked 25 cigarettes a day and that was just above his average killing for a day.

In those 12 years I was with him, he passed thru approximately 25 to 30 years. The first thing that happened was he set out to kill the entire family tree of those three men. He did this meticulously each time getting more information and learning to fight. He was brutal, children, women, old young nothing mattered. Eventually a group of very vicious men formed around him that group of men became an army. There are many things that came in-between and over time, he did soften a bit a very little bit. Never the less in the 12 years I was with him, I accomplished nothing at all; while in that time he formed an empire that stretched across Europe.

I saw so much fighting, killing, blood and some really undesirable ugly stuff that it goes beyond words. There where people so afraid of his armies that they would kill themselves in the battlefield just not to have to face his men. I think that says it all. Eventually he did die, as we all will some time. Now I don't know exactly why this all came about but there was some things that did happen as a result of it. To a certain extent, I became him and in some ways, he became me. I think that he was having dreams of my life, which was troubling him for years. The irony of it was that my life was as ugly to him as his was to me. I believe from what I have gathered he saw me as a coward who let people push him around and who worked for someone else for meager pay and so on. Well in 1999, I would almost have made him proud but in the end, I did not follow thru with it and so I will let that part of the story die.

The other thing that came from this was some knowledge of energy spots or power spots or what some call energy vortexes. He used these energy spots on a regular basis when fighting a battle and would do everything possible to fight the battle over these energy spots. An old sorcerer in the hills showed this to him and taught it to him and also to me at the same time, over a period of time. It was his work with those vortexes that I ended up in his life and he in mine. The energy in these vortexes gave him a huge advantage. The rumor was like this he would take 10,000 men, fight an army of 40,000 men, and win with few casualties. The survivors of the 40,000 men would say that they saw that they where fighting 50,000 to 60,000 men but there where only 10,000 men.

Unfortunately, he saw only one purpose for these vortexes and or energy spots but I saw something else. If he had not mess around with those vortexes, I would not have been dragged into his time line, into his life and I would not have understood what makes sending love so powerful and so dangerous for some that they would do anything to stop people from knowing about it.

But this is not all of it. I'm not going into it all but because of these vortexes I came in contact with another self of mine and he made this one look like a candy ass. I will explain that later.

Reach for the light

I find it amazing how our lives resemble trees
We stretch out trying to reach the light and touch
the sun
But our roots go deep and are entangled in the
Past, future, present, past lives and of course each
other
It seems that we keep on going around in circles
Continually facing our fears, hate, angers
Until we manage to turn them into Love

10

I decided I needed a break and it seemed that Sally and Ed needed it also. So, I told them that I'm going for a short walk and give Roody some exercise. I figured that Ed and Sally needed some time to absorb everything anyway.

While I was outside walking around and playing with Roody, I thought about what I had told Sally and Ed and if I should be telling what I had so far. I was leaving some things out and I had changed part of the story. I worry about what I write and how it will affect others. For a long time now, all I wanted was to live on a sailboat and be a treasure hunter. Not for the gold or the money but for the wonder of it, wondering how the stuff got there and who made it and so on. Maybe once all this is over and I have finished my books then I can live that dream, but then I remembered why I had that dream. It was to get away from all of this and all the things that happened. Walking back to the restaurant, I made a wish. I wished to have some of that wonder back some of the wonder I had as a kid before everything else happened. But then I realized that all of this started when I was a kid.

As Roody and I came back in the restaurant Sally was just refilling the bowl of water for Roody where he had been laying before we went for a walk.

"I thought that he might want some fresh water after his walk" said Sally.

Roody lapped up most of the water and then proceeded to continue his nap.

As I sat back, down on my stool Ed asked me if I wanted anything. I said some pop or something would be fine.

Sally was petting Roody and having a one-way conversation with him. As Ed placed a glass of pop in front of me he remarked, that I had a troubled look on my face. I just nodded my head, and said that I was just tired of it all and wanted to finish writing it out and be done with it all and preferably have people just leave me alone. But none of that will happen it will never end as soon as I figure out one thing and write it another thing comes up and the whole thing just starts all over again. And then there's the fear of being totally insane and not even knowing it and worst of all I could be leading others down the path of my insanity. In one way, I know I am doing the right thing but sometimes I just worry. You can't help but worry even if you cared only a little you would worry to. Sometimes the emotions of what if just hit me. At one time I use to wonder why me from all the people why me? Then I was shown why me. That was a shock. But at the same time, I already knew it; I just did not want to accept it.

"What do you mean" Asked Sally

I looked at Ed because I had the feeling he already put it together.

Well Ed", I said

Ed looked at Sally and then said. "I think that somewhere past, future, past life or probable life whatever he is somehow at least in part responsible for the reason that people have forgotten about the power we have and how to use it".

Sally looked at me with something of an I am sorry look and asked "Is that right"?

"Well would it not make sense? I answered and continued with I think we will leave it at that I would prefer it that way. I mean its rather a pile of shit isn't it on one end I have a self killing people by the thousands and using the vortexes to empower his armies. On the other end I have a self who is working to keep millions of people enslaved, I don't even care what the reasons are, and God only knows how many more similar ones of myself doing the same thing.

We sat in silence for some time. Then I went about explaining how things work as far as past selves, probable selves and so on. What we discussed is what is written in the beginning of this book under the heading (A few words before we start).

Closing time came for the restaurant and I gave them some time to lock up and shut down the kitchen at which point Sally had remarked that she has never seen the restaurant so quiet. Just another one of those coincidences, Na I think not.

It took them about a half an hour to close up and clean up. After it was all done, I realized that I should have maybe offered to help but I had been in deep thought and in some way felt like a burden had been lifted off my shoulders. Now as I write this, I feel the same way. There's one more piece left though and its this little piece that it was all about. It's this piece of knowledge that is causing such an uproar in places and worlds that most people only fantasize about existing. Some are excited and some are afraid for there very existence but only because they don't understand what's going to happen. Its one thing for people to know about it and another for them to use it, it will happen regardless of what is dun to stop it. The prophecy is in hand and it will be no matter what. The meek will inherit the earth and the skies the galaxies and universes. What people misunderstood was that it was thought to mean that the meek of the earth would inherit this but it is all the people of earth that will inherit this. What follows is the key as to how and why. You will see what I am saying shortly and you will most likely see more then just the beginnings of it in your lifetime.

Ed and Sally sat down after closing up and proceeded to bombard me with questions but I was not that forth coming. I prefer that people come up with there own answers. Most of the questions that come up while you read this book can be easily answered if you just step back a bit and seriously look at it.

You can tell when you have understood something because it will feel like you have remembered it sort of like saying O' I know that, I just did not see it. As you read that last piece here you will feel like O' you know it all along but just did not remember.

"So here is the rest of it the part that is really important," I said to Ed and Sally the fact that I'm here talking to you and that you are planning to go and live right at several large energy centers is quite the coincidence or is it? I asked smiling.

So lets take a look at these vortexes there is something very special about them. I said and continued. The thing about these vortexes is that they are timeless space in-between all the worlds in other words these vortexes are sort of doorways to anywhere in the universe and galaxies and best of all they are sort of doorways to all the probable worlds. Because we live in a framework of time we see things as past present and future and most people will in some way believe in past lives but in timeless space of existence all this happens at the same moment and it is the elusion of time that makes it look like one thing happens after another. So if you understood how to work those vortexes you could send a space ship in and come out at the edge of this universe instantly and could then fly around there looking at everything. Now this is where it gets tricky because you could in fact go back into the vortexes and come back here just minutes after you had left even though you spent weeks traveling around at that other place. It sounds like you are traveling back in time but you are just going thru a doorway and you are just choosing the doorway that opens at a place in time where you had just left. Do you see it?

"I think so" answered Ed, "totally" answered Sally that answers many questions.

"I think I get it answered ed so you could travel to another planet instantly and then come back the same way, the hard part I think would be finding the right doorway to the right probable world you came from".

"Bingo I answered but that's not where the magic is". I said excited that they could accept the probability of this being correct.

"It makes perfect sense because everything in the universe must be connected and so would have the connection points," answered Sally

That's right everything everywhere is connected thru these energy centers and there are billions upon billions of them all different sizes and shapes they can be as small as a pin head and as large as and larger then planets. There is much more to them and they are very fascinating but we are mostly interested in one thing. So now, we come to the fun part. If you could throw an apple into one just as an example of course, what you will get is not one apple coming out of the other end what you will have is one apple coming out of every vortex big enough to support that size. OK this will get some what confusing, See its like this those vortexes are timeless so in a sense they are everywhere at once. You can't just throw in an apple but if you know how to do it there would be an apple coming out of everyone of them. If you know, how you could also send in an apple and have it come out only one opening.

"I am having a hard time with this part," answered Ed.

I know that it is difficult to understand but science has already discovered that certain particles can be at different places at the same time. It like this if you can live different lifetimes then if you remove time then all those lifetimes are being lived all at the same time that means you are in more then one place at a time.

"I can sort of see it but it's hard to totally grasp," answered Sally and Ed was nodding his head.

"It does make sense but it is hard to fully understand," answered Ed.

I agree it took me a long time to get it myself but if you think about it in time, it starts to make sense. Let me give you some more on it. There are already scientists working on this as far as creating energy from those vortexes and it is done in the same way by sending in energy and trying to control where it comes out. The way the project works is that you send energy into one and then have it come out in lets just say 10 different vortexes because it will come out in the same amount you sent in; but in ten locations so in affect you have ten times the energy you sent in. They have had a lot of success with it but the problem was and still is, is controlling where it comes out because if it comes out somewhere where you do not have something to recapture the energy you have a live wire dangling in mid air that's just a metaphor it's a lot more serious then that.

So now comes the biggy. So you have come to understand what power we have when it comes to what we for now call sending love for lack of better word for it.

"O' yes answered Sally.

Ok then so if you sending love can have an affect to your life and also affect what happens to others and to the world as a hole. Then what would happen if I where to tell you that for some reason if you send love into those energy centers it automatically comes out at every-one of them all over the place. Listen I'm saying everywhere here and at every planet in all the galaxies and everywhere on this planet and on all the probable worlds it comes out at the same level you send it in at, it comes out at the same amount at all of them at the same time same moment. Think about the implications. The meek will inherit the earth. Well there was a piece left out the meek will inherit everything, and for one reason and one reason only because the power that created all life flows thru us and can be directed to where ever we want. This it the part that others wanted to stop so desperately because they do not understand this thing we call love and think that people will rule the worlds and galaxies and so control them but that's not the way love works. You can go to the farthest regions of the galaxies and to some whatever populated planet and there you will find prophesies of a peo-ple who come from nowhere and will change the face of all that was created. Everywhere you go you will find these prophesies some feel joy and some feel it will be there destruction. You know how things can get turned around to some what will become their joy can be seen as their death. Telling you what power lies in you the power that you have sitting in you ready to go to work for you to create heaven on earth and everywhere else is the most dangerous thing you can imagine telling you how to do it with the vortexes has meant a death sentence in the past for many.

Let me explain it to you this way. I do not know the exact number of vortexes on this planet but lets just say it is one million. What that means is that if you send love every day and also send that love into the vortex's just once it will come out at a million different places all over the world, That's a million times what you sent out. Listen when I was first shown this I fell off my chair but I had already studied these vortexes and had done some things with them. In my first book, I talk about how I traveled into the future and got the sports lottery results what I did not tell you was that I was also using one of those vortexes to do that. Therefore, I understood what those vortexes were capable of and when I was given this piece of information then the whole thing came together.

Now think about this do you really believe that god made you in his likeness and did not give you a connection to his creative power to create beauty and love wherever we go. What did you think was meant when he created man onto his likeness did you think that meant looks? Get real! It means you have the infinite spark of life and love in you waiting to be released.

Some of you will wonder why it was hidden from you and why anyone would want to try to stop it if that is what you think then you need to wake up to what is going on around you. Why would those in power and those that have control, why would they want you to find out that you are in control you have the power in you? This is not something they would want. Their way of life will end but before that happens, they will fight to the end to stop it. Tell me honestly that the wars you have fought and died in were for the goodness of the people or just for the vanity and power of a few. Do those few really want you have the power to stand up and say no to their ways. Do you think that someone on other planets that hunger for power would want you to have the power to change there ways of life whether it kills and enslaves millions of lives. It is nothing to them that is what they know and want. There are also many planets with beings of a different nature on them that want this to happen and have given their lives to protect this earth and the people on it otherwise we would not be here. Love does not control another but it has the power to stop the control of another.

I will say this in not such a nice way but if you cant even see the possibility that what I have told you is a possibility of the truth then you really are asleep and are wasting my time and millions of peoples lives who have given their lives protecting you so you could fulfill the prophesies. There are other beings out there who are finding that they also have these abilities but it seems that humans have the greatest ability in the regard to sending and releasing love. This is rather ironic considering mankind has been slaves for a long time and several times have been bred like cattle to be slaves. But it seems that is how the creator works, for in the end it is the meek who will inherit the earth. For all that was done to humans they did not realize that they were creating a super race of beings that would transform all that was created. Humans have been mutilated so bad that many wars have been fought just for entertainment like a chessboard. I know this is hard to take but all the evidence is there for you to see all you need to do is look at it. Some of you who believe that aliens have been coming here especially now, can you see why we are getting so much attention and the prophets told you of a great destruction but it did not happen. What was not told was that others where trying to destroy us in order to destroy the prophecy, a prophecy that is told in endless forms in endless worlds. Some of what you would call aliens have taken genetic samples and other things from humans in order to reinstall the ability to work with love in their race of people and are having some success. However, it is we humans who are the masters at it.

Now one more thing you might wonder why me that is an easy one. In other probabilities, I was working on the other side working very hard at stopping this information from getting out and I was very successful at it. When I first found out how dark, my dark side is I wanted to end my life. Your imagination cannot know how far that part of me has gone to stop this and to what price and cost. He is not alone of course but a part of it a large part of it. It is as unimaginable as it is bearable. In time, I understood why and how and by that time, he had almost turned me with him. Almost, so you can see its sort of fitting that I write this. Depending whether or not you can get the drift of this will depend on which prophecy will rule the next 2000 years.

Last Word

At this time I cannot give you exact instructions. If you have the will you will discover it. It's your destiny.

You can send love into any of these vortexes just pick the one that feels best, and all you need to do is add your intent that it should come out everywhere. That is all no effort at all. I know it sounds to easy, yes it does, I did not make up the rules I just found them. The more you look at all of this the more you can see that it was all set up. Regardless it works. The rest will come to you; somehow, it will be shown to you. It would take a whole book just on the instructions for them to be detailed out. The information is in you and will come to the surface as you start; it is like a capsule and as soon as people start to think about it and do something with it begins to open. There are also many other things that can be done with those vortexes.

Now many people have asked me about other things like praying. Of course praying will work, what do you think is happening while you are praying. Your heart opens and you send love. See that is the nice thing about sending love you can add it to almost every thing you do. If you love to pray for something then why not add sending love to it. Now if you pray in a form that does not open your heart and release love then there will be no results its that simple. It does not matter what religion you have or practice or what other things you enjoy just add opening and sending love to it and you will see a big difference to it. So you can dance around the fire under the moon like my wife does with her friends and as long as you open and send love while your doing this it will work for you like never before.

The meek will inherit the earth and now you know how and why.

All my love Klaus

Warrior

Warrior fighter of broken dreams
He will not slay the dragon
But
Faces his strength with love
Eye thru eye they combine their strength
And repair the broken dreams
United they become one
The dragons fire
The warriors love
As one
Make our dreams beautiful
And unlocks the secrets to the
Universe

—Roberta Joehle

Our Trees

When I was younger, most of if not all of my time was spent with the trees on the far side of the lake. Where no one ever went but me, they said that part of this great forest was haunted. I saw only love as I drew my sword and spent my entire day's sword fighting with these beautiful Trees. My only true friends. They taught me to fight and defense with out harm. To stand for what no one else would. To believe in what others only laughed at. The days went by so beautifully as my pain of loneliness was never in sight there. One day my bags where packed for me and shortly I arrived without my consent on the other side of the world. Here the Trees did not understand what I was trying to do. They where different, younger and without that ancient wisdom. My heart broke, my tears flowed for years. As I became older and taught some Trees here what I learned from the old ones. My heart began to heal. Now thirty-four years later I have heard from those that make no sound, speak no language that they are dying by the thousands. They have chosen to leave. Will there be time to see them again? Probably not for I have other duties to attend to. What a fool I have been to think that they would be there forever.

So I feel, as a piece of my heart dies with them.

Klaus J Joehle

Conclusions

What we have forgotten is to create with love
Not with
Our egos, thoughts, fears or beliefs,
But with Love
Or perhaps better said
I had forgotten

About the Author

Klaus was born in 1957 in Black Forest Germany. At age nine and still with the wonderful idea that Canada was the wild west, where Cowboys and wagon trails still existed; Klaus was sent to live with is aunt and uncle in Rosedale, British Columbia, Canada.

Klaus has now completed writing four books; this is the fourth and the sequel to his "extraordinary" first title *Living on Love "The Messenger"*. When he is not sailing his classic seventeen-foot boat "The Scurvy Dog" he continues to write and will bring you more wonderful books.

♥

Instructions

These instructions are going to be short and simple. In fact, to simple for the journey, you are going to undertake. If you take this journey threw the power of love like I have explained to you in as sending love you will be safe and it will be a journey of self discovery, Of Joy of self empowerment. You will feel as if you have come home but in fact you will just come to the knowing that you had never left home only shut down the flow of the creator and of love and joy. This journey will be different for everyone and even those that go together will discover treasures different from others, for the wonders of the creator are endless. Each must take that journey in there own way un-judged by another and un-led by another. You cannot follow the leader but each of you must follow your own joy un-led by another. So as you can see I nor anyone else can give you a road map to follow. Some will try, follow them not, follow your own joy and by that you will follow the creator in you of you and that you are. You can speak of the treasures you find there but leave others to find their own. There can be no gold on an island but 10 people can find treasure there. One will find it in the sand another will find it sleeping under a palm tree another in the worm waters.

There can be no map, but instead I will tell you that the island is there and how you will find the map in you. Your map your joy your love and your creator in what ever form he she may appear to you. Would you accept any thing less? Just as we, each experience the flow of sending love differently so you will experience what is to follow each to his or here own.

This is one of many ways to interact with the energy centers or vortexes. They come in all sizes and shapes the trick is not necessary to go after the biggest one but the ones that resonate with you. These energy centers are everywhere and you do not need to be next to them. Physically you could be a thousand miles away from them and still interact with them as if you are there and at times it can even work better if you are not physically right there. You will know what is right for you because you will feel it and you will sense that they are reacting to you and opening as a flower opens to the sun. Also, your heart will also open in the same way. As you interact with them with your heart, you can feel many things like a feeling of going home or an inner connection as if you have found an old friend. Its simple, if it feels good then you are working with the right one, if its not giving you joy then leave it use the feeling of joy to guide you.

How to find them!

Again this is just one of a thousand ways. While opening your heart imagine you are an eagle, the love coming from you is creating wings a thousand feet across. Just see yourself gliding across places where you are looking passing throw buildings trees and so on then just let your self feel the energy centers like a feather brushing along your wings. You can just go from one to the next until you find the one that feels right for you. Now if you want you can send love into it and with your intend you can direct it to come out in thousands of those energy centers all over the world and any where you want. The rest of what you can do will come to you in the form of intuition and ideas of fun. As I said, the journey will be different for everyone.

Only as a suggestion, it would still be best for you to send love into your life as a priority and do this, as it feels fun and interesting for you. You do not need to be in a deep state of mind for this a simple daydream will suffice very nicely.

All I can say is if you follow what gives you joy you will be following your highest good.

All my love Klaus